Profile of a Hit Songwriter

by

Lacie Carpenter

and Thornton Cline

ISBN 978-1-57424-382-6

P. O. Box 17878 - Anaheim Hills, CA 92817

email: centerstream@aol.com • **web:** centerstream-usa.com

714-779-9390

Acknowledgments

A special thank you
to Ted Perlman

Stephen Wrench

Ron Middlebrook and
Centerstream Publishing

Jan Buckingham

Hal Leonard Publishing

Michael Garvin

Mr. Burt Bacharach

Jenny Slate Lee

Lacie Carpenter

Michael Jay

Thornton Cline

Michele Vice-Maslin

Allan Rich

Tom Snow

Mark Oliverius

Dr. Jason Kastner

Jud Friedman

Leah Hudson

Paul Williams

John Bush

Tony Conliff

Wil Nance

Jerry Vandiver

Bart Herbison

Wayne Moss

Sue Main

Dee Moeller Moss

Becky Buller

Edy Nathan

Dr. Denise Stuart

Table of Contents:

Introduction

So, you want to write hit songs or at least you're considering it. Perhaps you've tried your hand at it but you're not sure if you've got what it takes to become a hit songwriter. You may have bought this book because it caught your attention about the profiling of a hit songwriter, and you were curious about what the characteristics and traits of a successful songwriter looked like. Maybe you believe that it's all luck, hard work, inspiration, politics or meeting the right people. Some of that is true, but there is a whole lot more to becoming a hit songwriter than meets the eye.

If you believe that age has something to do with success as a hit songwriter, you're in for a surprise. Sure, there have been some very young successful top-charting songwriters who started at an early age. But there have been some hit songwriters who either didn't start writing or achieving major successes until after the age of 30. According to *Billboard* magazine, songwriter, Rachel Platten didn't have her first hit until the age of 34. Her song, "Fight Song" climbed to the top of the *Billboard* Charts and brought her instant fame. It was also a popular worldwide TV theme song advertisement for the Target stores and was certified platinum.

Hit artist and songwriter, Sheryl Crow was a music teacher for autistic children and a background vocalist in her twenties. *All Music* says that at age 32, Crow had her first worldwide hit she co-wrote, "All I Wanna Do." It reached number two for six weeks on the **Billboard** Hot 100 Chart. She won a Grammy Award for Record of the Year and Best Female Pop Vocal Performance in 1995.

Famed songwriter, Leonard Cohen didn't release his debut album until age 33. Before that he was writing poems and literature. He moved to the United States from Canada in 1967 and released his first album, "Songs of Leonard Cohen." Seventeen years later at age 50, Cohen released his hit, "Hallelujah" which has been recorded by over 200 artists in different languages. He was honored with the Grammy Lifetime Achievement Award in 2010. His achievements to success are documented in the book, "Various Positions: A Life of Leonard Cohen" on Pantheon Books.

There are, of course, hit songwriters who are born with the gift of writing at a very early age. But that is not generally the norm. Most hit songwriters are older, and more seasoned. As you will learn later in this book, age doesn't really matter when it comes to becoming a hit songwriter. It has more to do with what the hit songwriter is made of—his or her profile. But back to the hit songwriters who made it at an early age, the four who come to mind are: Lorde, Adele, Stevie Wonder and Dolly Parton.

Lorde, whose real name is Ella Marija Lani Yellich-O'Connor, is the youngest singer to have a US number one **Billboard** hit in 26 years. She was 16-years-old when she became the first solo artist from New Zealand to achieve a number one single in the US with a song, she wrote solo, "Royals" according to *Time* magazine. The National Academy of Recording Arts and Sciences honored Lorde with two Grammy Awards in 2014. She became the youngest ever in music history to win, "Song of the Year."

British hit artist and songwriter, Adele (born Adele Laurie Blue Adkins) had her first major success at age 19 with critically-acclaimed songs she wrote for her debut album, "19." *Rolling Stone* magazine reported that her hit song, "Hometown Glory" was written at 16-years-old. The album was certified platinum seven times in the UK and three times platinum in the US. In 2009, Adele was awarded a Grammy for Best New Artist and Best Female Pop Vocal Performance.

Gifted singer-songwriter-actress, Dolly Parton wrote her first top-ten **Billboard** hit song at age 20, "Put it Off Until Tomorrow." Parton came from a family of 12 children and began singing solo performances in her church at age six. When she was seven-years-old, Parton taught herself to

Introduction

play guitar. In 2001, she was inducted into the Songwriters Hall of Fame. Parton has written over 3,000 tunes and started writing seriously at age seven. She has been honored with numerous Academy Awards, Grammy Awards and CMA Awards. All of Parton's great achievements can be found at *Biography.com*

In 1963, legendary singer-songwriter, Stevie Wonder (born Stevland Hardaway Judkins) had his first hit **Billboard** number one charted song called "Fingertips." He was only 12-years-old when he wrote the hit. Many music critics have referred to him as a "child prodigy" and a "genius" as he made his recording debut at age 11. Wonder first showed his gift when he sang in his church choir at age four and later went on to teach himself the harmonica, piano and drums, all before age ten. Stevie Wonder has had many number one hits, Grammy Awards and was inducted into the Rock and Roll Hall of Fame in 1989. See *Biography.com* for more details.

Age is just a number when it comes to becoming a hit songwriter. There are exceptions to the rule with child prodigies and geniuses. The "Talent Code" by Daniel Coyle tells us that it takes 10,000 hours to master a skill. There are exceptions for everything. There was boy, Mozart, who was writing his first composition at four-years-old. He couldn't have possibly trained in writing music for 10,000 hours. For every fact or rule, there is a counter rule. For everyone who says it can't be done, there are people who show the world that it can be accomplished.

In this book we will make the case, through research, years of experience, and interviews, that it's the profile of the hit songwriter—the right stuff that really matters. Sure, factors such as environment, luck, hard work (10,000 hours), politics and meeting the right people have important effects on writing hit songs, but not as much as you would think. It really comes down to who you are and what you're made of. Are you ready to discover your traits, characteristics and the core of who you truly are? Read on and keep an open mind. You are about to make an important discovery of what makes a hit songwriter.

Chapter One:
The Scope of This Book

By the time you have finished this book, you will have discovered the necessary personality traits and characteristics hit songwriters possess—laying aside the influential external factors such as environment, luck, hard work, politics and networking with the decision makers.

You will have read the interviews of successful hit songwriters we have selected who live in the major music centers of the world. They cover a broad spectrum of musical genres and share valuable information about what components they possess from birth to their current status in life. All have been asked the same questions about the following topics: self-discipline, self-esteem, passion, drive (energy and stamina), work ethic, focus (detail and perfectionism), belief (faith), resilience (patience and practice), curiosity, mental attitude (optimism, doers and positivity), risk-taking, personal care, being a visionary and a dreamer, commitment (goal setting—short and long-term), being resourceful, learning from failure, continuing to learn, obsession and learning to stand your ground (saying no).

Also included are the interviews of successful hit music producers representing the major music cities. They share their perspective on the traits and characteristics of hit songwriters based on the topics asked above.

Interviews on the same subjects are provided by successful songwriter coaches-teachers and by the authors of this book, Lacie Carpenter and Thornton Cline.

Research into the lives, traits, and characteristics of some of the great, legendary songwriters of yesteryear are explored. A section of how environment plays a role in hit songwriting is addressed: upbringing, musical influences, family, friends, financial means and mentors.

This book would not be complete without interviewing some expert psychologists who work with hit songwriters in the major music cities for their perspective on what internal traits and characteristics make up a hit tunesmith. These psychological and neurological experts are asked to respond to the same above-mentioned points.

Since early childhood development is so important to the success of adults later in life, we decided to interview some pediatricians to get their perspective on how children can develop into hit songwriters. Again, we will explore external factors, natural gifts and talents, and characteristics and traits of children to determine what might lead a child to become a hit songwriter.

It seemed appropriate to wrap up the book with a self-evaluation questionnaire of the specific topics addressed by the professional—but completed by you, the aspiring songwriter, so you could determine if you have what it takes to get to the top in songwriting.

Chapter Two:

Interview with Producer/Songwriter **Mark Oliverius**

Hit producer/songwriter, **Mark Oliverius**

Mark Oliverius brings a musical acumen to the studio that few in the industry can match.

Mark is a Yamaha Instruments Endorsed Nashville music producer/songwriter/keyboard player who has produced over 200 recording projects and has spent a career touring with numerous big-name recording artists for the last 32 years.

In addition to his role as Director of Music for many projects, Mark was also Lorrie Morgan's music director for 18 years. He has had over 40 cuts as a songwriter including recordings by Mickey Gilley, Pam Tillis, Sawyer Brown, Trick Pony, Lorrie Morgan, Sammy Kershaw, Burns & Poe, T.G. Sheppard, Ethan Bortnick, Kelly Lang and he wrote a hit for Joe Diffie. His Production credits include Lorrie Morgan, Pam Tillis, Burns & Poe, The Dallas Cowboys, Ashton Shepherd, Rio Grande, Cowboy Troy, Ashlee Hewitt, P.J. Anderson, Katie Armiger, and Veronica Ballestrini, etc.

Mark has expertise in producing, arranging, writing, programming, leading world-class musicians in great studio environments and on stage; in addition to being an experienced videographer and film editor.

Mark's skillful interpretation and masterful arrangements give all projects he involves himself with the presence of a nationally-produced commercial sound. With a keen eye and ear for rising talent and unique style, Mark is instrumental in discovering the up-and-coming artists that are a part of The Music of Nashville® cast.

For Mark, it all starts with passion. When Mark Oliverius, Bob Walker and Candace Lucchesi put their heads together about how to accomplish the creation of The Music of Nashville® A Magical Journey, they were determined to bring to fruition their dream of presenting a larger than life musical performance. Auditions took place in Nashville November of 2016, and the team hasn't stopped since. Between pre-production, photo shoots, video shoots, recording, rehearsals, and series of shows, The Music of Nashville® has exploded with growth.

Do you believe drive, passion, and stamina (energy level) play a major role in helping a person to become a successful hit songwriter?

Absolutely! A songwriter must have the drive and stamina to outwork and out write all the other songwriters looking for cuts. You always have to believe in yourself and your art.

Do you think work ethic plays a vital part in becoming a hit songwriter? If so, how?

You must outwork the rest of the field. Luck also plays a large role.

Interview with Producer/Songwriter **Mark Oliverius**

How much does faith and belief in one's abilities help in becoming a hit songwriter?

Again, you have to have faith in your instincts...to create a song that resonates with John Q. Public.

How much of focus to detail and perfection helps make a hit songwriter?

Everything about the lyric and recording has to feel great..thus..attention to detail.

What role does commitment to short and long-term goals affect success as a hit songwriter?

Writing is a long game. No quick payoffs.

Do you believe that learning from failures and rejections help in becoming a hit songwriter? Please elaborate.

Failures make you stronger...you realize that you're the only one who believes in you...you learn to trust your gut and instincts.

Do you feel like being obsessive and persistent with writing help in becoming a successful hit songwriter? If so, how?

You have to work hard at it...but...sometimes the muse isn't there.

Do you think taking risks in your career has helped you become successful? If so, how?

Yes...taking risks makes one a true leader.

Do you believe having a positive mental attitude, being optimistic, and possessing strong self-esteem play a major role in success? If so, how?

Yes, optimism grows out of a series of small victories... being kind and helping people is a great mindset to have.

Does being a doer and not a talker help in becoming successful? If so, how?

Few do. Many talk. Who has the resume?

Does being a visionary or a dreamer help artists become successful? If so, how?

You always have to look outside the boundaries...as opposed to copying...create something FRESH!

Do you think overall personality contributes to the success of a songwriter? If so, how?

Drive, passion, brains, fortitude, brains, fortitude, brains.

Do you feel patience and practice play a role in the creation of a hit songwriter?

Yes...writing every day gets a person focused on structure and word flow. Inspiration still has to play a major role.

How much prioritizing your life from day-to-day helps you become successful?

Setting deadlines for everything you do will help you work within a given timeline.

Do you continue to learn all you can about your profession? If so, how?

Of course. I study and practice all the time, from watching videos on mixing, filmmaking, programming to practicing and running two shows...stay in MOTION!

Interview with Producer/Songwriter **Mark Oliverius**

In any part of your life, has self-discipline played a major role in helping become successful? If so, how?

Working and improving and learning all of the time... you have to outwork the competition.

Is there any factor, trait, or ingredient we may have omitted that helps in becoming a successful, hit songwriter?

Fearlessness, perseverance, melody.

Do you believe a hit songwriter is born or made? Explain your thoughts.

Mostly born. A person either has the "Muse" or not.

Do you believe talent is a gift or is it earned? Explain your thoughts.

Talent is a gift. The betterment and development of that talent is earned through sweat equity.

Do you believe that talent comes from within? If so, is it how they process stimuli in life?

Talent is a way of expressing oneself uniquely...It is created by and a reflection of the environment around you.

What is talent?

The ability to excel, reach and touch people through art, athletics or any other activity. Having a very unique skill set.

Do you believe self-criticism helps or harms the success of a hit songwriter?

Every artist critiques his or her work...it is essential to artistic growth.

Do you believe hit songwriters are more attuned to what is going on and happening around them than others?

Yes...it's the role of the songwriter to absorb cultural phenomena and explain it in three minutes!

Hit producer/songwriter, **Mark Oliverius** pictured with the cast of his live hit show, *"The Music of Nashville."*

Chapter Three:

Interview with Songwriter **Allan Rich**

Allan Rich is a two-time Academy Award, Grammy and Golden Globe nominee, whose songs have sold over 65 Million copies.

Allan has written hits for everyone from: NATALIE COLE ("I Live For Your Love")JAMES INGRAM (the #1 pop hit "I Don't Have The Heart To Hurt You")WHITNEY HOUSTON ("Run To You" from the movie "The Bodyguard" which sold 30 Million CD's and got Allan his first Oscar and Grammy nomination)KENNY LOGGINS ("For The First Time" from the Michelle Pfeiffer/ George Clooney movie "One Fine Day" which got Allen another Oscar, Grammy and Golden Globe nomination)'NSYNC ("I Drive Myself Crazy" from their 10 million selling debut CD)....as well as songs recorded by BARBRA STREISAND, TINA TURNER, ROD STEWART, LUTHER VANDROSS, DOLLY PARTON, PATTI LA BELLE, GLADYS KNIGHT. BARRY MANILOW....and many others!

Do you believe drive, passion, and stamina (energy level) play a major role in helping a person to become a successful hit songwriter?

I think it's equally important as talent. Maybe even more important than talent. I have known several songwriters who were so gifted, but they couldn't put up with the constant rejection, and they eventually gave up writing. That always saddened me. Because I felt if they had stuck it out they would have made it. But making a living as a songwriter is not for the meek. I have always asked myself, "How bad do you want it?" And I wanted it bad enough to survive the bullets of rejection that come at you on a daily basis. Don't get me wrong; there were times I didn't get out of bed for a day or two and still don't when I felt I hit it out of the ballpark and my song is "passed" on. But I have always tried to turn lemons into lemonade. And passion and the desire to move and touch people has always been my driving force.

Do you think work ethic plays a vital part in becoming a hit songwriter? If so, how?

Everybody works differently. But it takes 24/7 every day to get better, improve and break through. It's not just about writing though. It's about going to see artists, meeting publishers, and producers. It's about networking, networking, networking. I have always beat myself up because I have a short attention span. My writing partner, Jud Friedman can sit there all day and work. He always jokes and says, "I know you've had a long day. You've worked three hours!" LOL! It is funny, and it is true for me. But even when I'm not writing, I'm processing. I'm thinking. I fool myself into writing, without feeling like I am. If I get one crucial line in a song in one day, I feel like I've succeeded. But for 10 years, Jud and I worked 5 days a week, all day long. And we loved it.

Interview with Songwriter **Allan Rich**

How much does faith and belief in one's abilities help in becoming a hit songwriter?

There's a lot of blind faith involved. I always put it out in the universe that I'm going to succeed. But I just don't know how it's going to happen! But I just have to believe that something special's going to come my way if I do my work. I just have to continue to put it out there. And it only takes one champion. With that said, I can be a real pessimist and doubt myself. But like a song, Jud and I wrote "I Choose to Believe" in spite of it all.

How much of focus to detail and perfection helps make a hit songwriter?

One word, one note, one production sound can change EVERYTHING! And one should strive to be meticulous, and go over the lyric and music, and the production with a fine-tooth comb. Don't settle. However, sometimes when you're working on a project, and there's a deadline, you just have to let it go and not be so precious. But sloppy shows in a song. You can't hide it. Now I am not a poet and I don't write very flowery. I call myself a "missionary position" songwriter, LOL, because I am a traditional songwriter. I try to write a lyric that is a simple, real conversation between two people; something that you could hear yourself saying in the situation. Or something you could overhear between two people. And within that simplicity, I try to add a twist and make the lyric heartfelt and fresh.

What role does commitment to short and long-term goals affect success as a hit songwriter?

On one hand, you can only take it one minute, one hour, one day at a time, Cause, otherwise, you can drive yourself crazy. But on the other hand, you do need a long-term goal so that you end up being able to be a songwriter through the good and bad times. And you need a good team around you. Don't get me wrong, I'm thankful that I'm doing just fine. But if I had to do it all over again, I would take my career more seriously as a businessman. There was a lot more money in the pipeline that I'm sure I didn't get. And I should have kept better records, files for each song, splits, etc. And I should've had a better understanding of the business side of the music industry.

Do you believe that learning from failures and rejections help in becoming a hit songwriter? Please elaborate.

You can sometimes learn more from the failures than from the successes. But I much prefer the successes in my career.

Do you feel like being obsessive and persistent with writing help in becoming a successful hit songwriter? If so, how?

Obsession and persistence are necessary in order to succeed. But sometimes the obsessiveness blocks your creativity. You want it so bad! Well, that can stress you out and lead to creative blocks. But you must have that intense desire in order to break through... where nothing else matters.

Do you think taking risks in your career has helped you become successful? If so, how?

My whole career has been about taking risks. I feel like "I Love Lucy" with all the crazy things I've done to get noticed and to get my songs heard and recorded. I could spend the whole interview just talking about all of them.

Do you believe having a positive mental attitude, being optimistic, and possessing strong self-esteem play a major role in success? If so, how?

You have to BELIEVE you can succeed. But some of

my best, most successful songs have been based on my vulnerabilities. "Run to You" from The Bodyguard was written specifically for Whitney. But I was going through a 10-year breakup and used that pain to write the lyric. I was feeling bad about myself when I wrote the lyric to God to help me. It was called, "So Help Me God." Jud wrote the music and it was recorded by Ray Charles. I was so melancholy about how many friends had died of AIDS. I wrote a first-draft lyric, "We Will Meet Again," brought it to Brenda Russell, and we worked on it, and Oleta Adams cut it. Most of the time I get a "hit out of a heartache," LOL!

Does being a doer and not a talker help in becoming successful? If so, how?

I've always heard it said in the spiritual world not to defuse your idea or creativity by talking about it before it's done. It dilutes the power. Keep it to yourself. Do it first. Talk about it later.

Does being a visionary or a dreamer help artists become successful? If so, how?

If you're fortunate enough or brave enough to not care about what others think and forge your own path, good on you! I admire that so much. Visionary would not be a word to describe me. I don't think out of the box enough. I'm afraid to try a lot of new things and I care too much about what people think. But dreamer, absolutely. But both can lead to real success.

Do you think overall personality contributes to the success of a songwriter? If so, how?

Yes. As in all people businesses, and music is one, no one wants to work with an a...hole or someone who takes air out of the room. In collaborations, it's difficult to work with someone who only likes the sound of their own voice, or melody or lyric and is not open to yours.

Do you feel patience and practice play a role in the creation of a hit songwriter?

If I was a bodybuilder, it would take years to get the kind of body to be a professional. Same with songwriting. Unless you are born that gifted, you need years to improve your writing skills, improve your playing, and getting to a point where you are consistently writing on a high level. But even the best songwriters can write a mediocre song. We all have a few of those.

How much prioritizing your life from day-to-day helps you become successful?

I like living life while I'm songwriting. Even when I'm shopping in the mall. Or going grocery shopping, songwriting is always a priority and at the forefront of my mind. But you can't do songwriting half the way if you want to be a professional. It has to be a priority.

Do you continue to learn all you can about your profession? If so, how?

I'd say that continuing to learn is one of my shortcomings. But I do wish I could sit still longer, and learn more, especially about computers and electronics which are such an important part of the industry and being self-sufficient.

In any part of your life, has self-discipline played a major role in helping become successful? If so, how?

Discipline is very important in any field. You can't say you are a songwriter and then not write songs. And being a successful songwriter requires full-time attention. But there are times when lack of discipline can lead to real bursts of creativity. So, I'm a believer in both.

Is there any factor, trait, or ingredient we may have omitted that helps in becoming a successful, hit songwriter?

Compassion, empathy. That helps in moving and touching people in your songs.

Interview with Songwriter **Allan Rich**

Do you believe a hit songwriter is born or made? Explain your thoughts.

Both. Just like students in school, some have to work hard to get good grades while others excel naturally. But for most, a songwriter is made!! From years of sweat, tears, inspiration and personal experiences.

Do you believe talent is a gift or is it earned? Explain your thoughts.

I think talent is a gift that needs to be watered and nurtured in order to grow and bloom.

Do you believe that talent comes from within? If so, is it how they process stimuli in life?

Talent comes from within. But talent might be hidden and need to be uncovered. How many of us have found a talent we didn't think we had? And that we end up being really good at! If there's the slightest interest, then you should try your hand at it.

What is talent?

The definition of "talent" is natural aptitude or skill. But natural aptitude or skill is not enough. You need more than talent in order to succeed. Talent, combined with persistence and drive, desire and passion are the ingredients necessary to succeed. I've known real talents who haven't broken through because of their lack of passion or desire.

Do you believe self-criticism helps or harms the success of a hit songwriter?

There is a difference between self-criticism that is constructive and self-flagellation that is destructive. You need to be honest with yourself and your songs and whether they are the best they can be. But beating yourself up over it is counterproductive to your wellbeing in life. And takes the joy out of the journey. I am guilty of that. I know that from experience. You also have to be careful not to over analyze a song to the point that you take the magic out of the song.

Do you believe hit songwriters are more attuned to what is going on and happening around them than others?

I don't think they are necessarily more attuned to what's going on. But they are more attuned to accessing their feelings and emotions. And they're probably better observers of life and people. I love watching people. And overhearing their conversations. I get so many ideas from just being quiet and listening. I love being nosy! Lol!

Do you believe inspiration is a state of mind and could it be a major factor in the creation of a hit songwriter? Why?

I think inspiration is a state of mind. And it has to do with connecting to a higher power. If we listen carefully and are quiet inside, there are melodies and lyrics that the universe is giving us. We just have to be open to receiving it.

Chapter Four:

Interview with Producer / Songwriter **Stephen Wrench**

Hit songwriter and producer, **Stephen Wrench**, President of Musik and Film.

Stephen Wrench has performed the world over on stages in front of tens of thousands to "honky-tonks" in small towns. He has worked in many capacities including as artist manager, producer and VP of a major record label in Nashville. Stephen's first has always been as a creator of music, penning thousands of songs. For Stephen, it is all about evoking emotion through lyrics and music. Stephen has worked with as a former member, performer, producer or manager with the following artists: Lynyrd Skynyrd, Toto, Loverboy, Missing Persons, Bob Seger and The Silver Bullet, Eddie and the Cruisers, Dr. Hook, Atlanta Rhythm Section, Bad Company, Tommy Tutone, Survivor, Rick Springfield, John Anderson, David Allen Coe, Molly Hatchet, Blackfoot, Red Jumpsuit Apparatus, Ryan Starr, The Flamingos, Sister Hazel, Blessid Union of Souls, Craig Campbell, Grand Funk Railroad, ABBA, Chad Brock, Michael Peterson, Daryl Worley, Lonestar, and Collin Raye.

Do you believe drive, passion, and stamina (energy level) play a major role in helping a person to become a successful hit songwriter?

Yes, passion especially passion creates.

Do you think work ethic plays a vital part in becoming a hit songwriter? If so, how?

Yes, and if you do not work at it even though you are creative, the passion will never come out.

How much does faith and belief in one's abilities help in becoming a hit songwriter?

You have to believe in yourself or you will never present your work, and no one will ever hear your creations.

How much of focus to detail and perfection helps make a hit songwriter?

Create to perfection. Because if you do not pay attention to your creation it will not appeal to the masses.

What role does commitment to short and long-term goals affect success as a hit songwriter?

Sometimes a song comes out of nowhere, but most of the time it comes from an idea that is massaged and perfected.

Do you believe that learning from failures and rejections help in becoming a hit songwriter? Please elaborate.

Never give up and create for yourself.

Interview with Producer / Songwriter **Stephen Wrench**

Do you feel like being obsessive and persistent with writing help in becoming a successful hit songwriter? If so, how?

Yes, never give up and create for yourself.

Do you think taking risks in your career has helped you become successful? If so, how?

Yes, don't follow the rules or success will never come.

Do you believe having a positive mental attitude, being optimistic, and possessing strong self-esteem play a major role in success? If so, how?

Then you are not afraid to create.

Does being a doer and not a talker help in becoming successful? If so, how?

Of course, if you're a talker, you never create songs.

Does being a visionary or a dreamer help artists become successful? If so, how?

John Lennon said it all.

Do you think overall personality contributes to the success of a songwriter? If so, how?

It defines your creations.

Do you feel patience and practice play a role in the creation of a hit songwriter?

You may write a song that is just okay, but when you have the patience to refine it to a work of art, it becomes a great song.

How much prioritizing your life from day-to-day helps you become successful?

You have to dedicate time to your craft.

Do you continue to learn all you can about your profession? If so, how?

Yes, it is a craft, and a craft is practiced and perfected.

In any part of your life, has self-discipline played a major role in helping become successful? If so, how?

Discipline creates perfection.

Is there any factor, trait, or ingredient we may have omitted that helps in becoming a successful, hit songwriter?

Talent that you are born with. Music and songwriter are releasing the passion within the soul, and if the listener feels nothing, then you have created nothing. Writing a song can be done two ways. I have written some in five minutes as fast as the pen would move and then picked up a guitar and first music that came out, fit beautifully. Then I have painlessly worked on others for years. It's like a great voice, either it has it, or it doesn't.

Do you believe a hit songwriter is born or made? Explain your thoughts.

It is made from talented people that believe in themselves.

Do you believe talent is a gift or is it earned? Explain your thoughts.

Both-- talent is a gift, but without work ethic, it never becomes a hit song.

Interview with Producer / Songwriter **Stephen Wrench**

Do you believe that talent comes from within? If so, is it how they process stimuli in life?

From within, definitely. By creating their craft.

What is talent?

Uniqueness, and not being afraid to let your talent out to the world.

Do you believe self-criticism helps or harms the success of a hit songwriter?

Helps those who believe in themselves.

Do you believe hit songwriters are more attuned to what is going on and happening around them than others?

Yes and no. They just see things differently.

Do you believe inspiration is a state of mind, and could it be a major factor in the creation of a hit songwriter? Why?

Of course, you have to be inspired to create good material.

Do you believe having empathy helps in becoming a hit songwriter? Explain.

It is an emotion, and that is what songwriting is, expressing emotion.

Hit songwriter/producer, **Stephen Wrench** (right) pictured with American actor, **Tom Proctor** (left). Wrench and Proctor star in the new ABC-TV show, *"Son of an Outlaw."*

Chapter Five:

Interview with Songwriter **Jan Buckingham**

Hit songwriter, **Jan Buckingham**

Jan Buckingham is a twice Grammy nominated songwriter/producer/publisher/artist who has crafted hits for Whitney Houston, Melissa Manchester, Air Supply, Crystal Gayle, Clay Aiken, Lee Greenwood, Pam Tillis, George Jones, Tammy Wynette, Tim McGraw, Juice Newton, Gary Morris, Barbara Mandrell, Ronnie Milsap, the Nashville Pie Holes, Carvin/Walls and many more. Jan has also penned songs for many movies and television shows, including MY COUSIN VINNIE, A THING CALLED LOVE, HOLLYWOOD WIVES, and FRIENDS. Jan loves to perform (Nashville, LA, Branson, Gulf Shores, etc.) and helps many young writers and artists. Jan's BIO is at www.janbuckingham.com, and over 250 of Jan's current demos can be found at www.reverbnation.com/janbuckingham.

Do you believe drive, passion, and stamina (energy level) play a major role in helping a person to become a successful hit songwriter?

Yes. First, you have to love what you do. If you do love it, as I do songwriting, you'll do it (or think about it) 24 hours a day.... but if you have a job you hate, you'll do it 8 hours and come home and smoke, drink or watch TV, or possibly all three!! Also, I work out every day to keep my body feeling good and mind in top shape. I also eat well, and also eat a bit of protein before I write, as that is food for the brain.

Do you think work ethic plays a vital part in becoming a hit songwriter? If so, how?

Yes. I believe that one's work ethic plays a vital part in becoming a hit songwriter. I set aside time each day during the week to write. I schedule the writes just like sessions and are scheduled in Nashville, at 10 a.m., 2 p.m. and 6 p.m..... I used to write three songs a day, but now I am more balanced and go to the gym, then write, and at night relax or play out a various song venue here in Nashville. To me, that makes a perfect day!

How much does faith and belief in one's abilities help in becoming a hit songwriter?

I believe that faith and belief in one's abilities help a lot in becoming a hit songwriter. What you believe is the truth and the truth for you. If you believe you can, you can...If you believe you can't, you're right. And other people usually believe about you what you believe about yourself. I always told people I was a writer, and I believed that I was...and I visualized having success doing...and so that came to pass!!

Interview with Songwriter **Jan Buckingham**

How much of focus to detail and perfection helps make a hit songwriter?

I believe that focus to detail and perfection helps make a hit songwriter. Now, all songs that one writes will not be hits...but with each one; the writer gets better and better...Detail is very important...having the song be all in the same person and the same tense, having good visuals in the song, having the characters be true to their character and realistic in their responses...A song must be believable for a listener to relate to it.

What role does commitment to short and long-term goals affect success as a hit songwriter?

Commitments to long and short-term goals greatly affects the success of hit songwriters. Again, one must visualize what they see happening in their lives to make those things happen. It comes down to as simple an action as thinking, "I think I'll go in the kitchen and get a glass of water," and then doing that...Or, even, "I think I'll make a movie called the TITANIC," and then doing that...It all starts in the mind and what you visualize happening there, and then going out into the world and making it happen there...I always dreamed of writing hit songs.

Do you believe that learning from failures and rejections help in becoming a hit songwriter? Please elaborate.

Yes, learning from failures and rejections help one to become a hit songwriter. For every cut I've gotten, I'm sure I got dozens of rejections before the elusive "yes" was achieved...And once you make a mistake and suffer the consequences, you are certainly less likely to make that mistake again.

Do you feel like being obsessive and persistent with writing help in becoming a successful hit songwriter? If so, how?

Yes, I believe that being obsessive and persistent helps one to become a hit songwriter...Sometimes that behavior can be very frustrating, but over time, it pays off!! The old saying, "try, try again" is very true!!

Do you think taking risks in your career has helped you become successful? If so, how?

Yes, taking risks in my career has certainly helped me become successful!! One time, I went into the Soundstage and asked the secretary to give Jim Ed Norman, when he came out of the recording studio to use the restroom, a cassette, and this note: "Jim Ed, I know you have already started producing the Gary Morris/Crystal Gayle album...but do yourself a favor and listen to this song before you're done. Thank you, Jan Buckingham." Pretty ballsy, but it worked! Jim Ed called me the next day and told me he'd cut the song, and it turned out to be the title cut of the album: WHAT IF WE FALL IN LOVE.

Do you believe having a positive mental attitude, being optimistic, and possessing strong self-esteem play a major role in success? If so, how?

Yes, I certainly believe that having a positive mental attitude, being optimistic, and possessing a strong self-esteem play a major role in success! Again, people are going to believe about you what you show them that you believe about yourself. ..If you don't believe that a producer will cut your song, you'll never take the chance and pitch it to them...Also, nobody knows for sure, so if you act very confident about how good your song is, then the artist and/or producer will more than likely want to believe that too, as all of you want success!!!

Does being a doer and not a talker help in becoming successful? If so, how?

Yes, being a doer and not a talker helps one become successful. Talk is cheap and actions speak louder than words.

Interview with Songwriter **Jan Buckingham**

Does being a visionary or a dreamer help artists become successful? If so, how?

Yes, being a visionary and/or a dreamer helps artists become successful. I have a friend who knew Shania Twain long before she had any success, but my friend told me that from the get-go, Shania always saw herself singing in stadiums…and eventually, she did!!

Do you think overall personality contributes to the success of a songwriter? If so, how?

Yes, overall, personality contributes to the success of a songwriter. People like to work with people that they like to be around. That's a no brainer. Just like in LA, when I was acting, and at an audition, there would be ten women that all looked alike going out for the same role. Who gets the role? The one that the producers liked the best, who had a good personality and who would be the easiest to work with.

Do you feel patience and practice play a role in the creation of a hit songwriter?

Yes, patience and practice definitely play a role in the creation of a hit songwriter. Practice makes perfect, as they say. I have written thousands and thousands of songs…and only a hundred or so have been recorded. But I love to write. I do it all the time, and that is what pays off. You only get better and better. How much prioritizing your life from day-to-day helps you become successful believe you have to prioritize in your life, day by day, to achieve success. In my appointment book, I map out each day, always putting in time for the gym and a co-writer and a gig…and of course, making time for family…Once you realize what is really important to you, you make those things happen first…Oh, and if I have a job I dread; I do it first to get it over with and out of the way.

Do you continue to learn all you can about your profession? If so, how?

Yes, I continue to learn all I can about my profession. It has changed so much with the Internet and YouTube and streaming, etc. If you don't want to be left in the dust, you gotta keep up!!!

In any part of your life, has self-discipline played a major role in helping become successful? If so, how?

Self-discipline has played a major role in becoming successful in every part of my life…Going to the gym, writing thank-you notes, calling people back, being on time, etc. You have to make up your mind to do what you say you are going to do, so that people will trust you…and so that you can trust yourself!!!

Is there any factor, trait, or ingredient we may have omitted that helps in becoming a successful, hit songwriter?

The factor, trait of ingredient that you may have omitted in this questionnaire on how to be a successful songwriter would be that one must LOVE to write songs…That is the thing that keeps one doing it!!! With or without success, I have done it since I was eight years old…Sometimes I'm not and sometimes I'm not…but I'm always writing because I love to do it!!

Do you believe a hit songwriter is born or made? Explain your thoughts.

I believe you are born with certain traits…but to be successful at something, you have to work at it…So, a songwriter may be born to do it, but it won't happen unless the person works at writing those songs.

Do you believe talent is a gift or is it earned? Explain your thoughts.

"Talent" is kind of a gift, but it has to be developed… Just like a painter gets better and better the more be paints, and a singer gets better and better the more

Interview with Songwriter **Jan Buckingham**

he sings, and a plumber gets better and better the more he plumbs...Again, practice makes perfect...or at least better!!

Do you believe that talent comes from within? If so, is it how they process stimuli in life?

I believe that "talent" comes from within...In a way... You are born with things that interest you, or something affects you and sparks an interest. That interest then grows as one learns more about it...I also now tap into the mental internet all around me when I write, and "hear" in my head what I write down...That part is hard to explain, but the longer I've written, the faster I hear the things in my mind that I write down.

What is talent?

"Talent" is an ability to express oneself in a way that others can relate to.

Do you believe self-criticism helps or harms the success of a hit songwriter?

I believe that POSITIVE self-criticism can HELP a songwriter...I listen back to songs and think, "Geez, that could have been better if I had just said..." We're always improving, and we learn from our mistakes."

Do you believe hit songwriters are more attuned to what is going on and happening around them than others?

Hit songwriters maybe observe more than your average Joe, so that they can write about it...but on the other hand, we songwriters are often viewed as "spaced out," because we are always dreaming and creating, and sometimes miss what is right in front of us!! Every person on the planet is focused on something and because of that, misses something else.

Do you believe inspiration is a state of mind, and could it be a major factor in the creation of a hit songwriter? Why?

Inspiration is kind of a state of mind...and it IS a major factor in writing a hit song...but you have to be open to the inspiration...Sometimes it shows up when you have a schedule write, and sometimes it knocks you in the head when you least expect it...and you have to stop what you're doing and write it down right then, before it goes away...And I've learned the hard way that if I DREAM a melody or lyric, I better damned well get up and write it down and/or record it right then... because if I just go back to sleep, it may be gone in the morning!!!

Do you believe having empathy helps in becoming a hit songwriter? Explain.

Yes, I believe that empathy helps one become a hit songwriter...If you can't put yourself in the other person's shoes, how can you possibly write about how that person feels???

Chapter Six:

Interview with Songwriter / Producer / Artist **Michael Garvin**

Hit songwriter, artist, and producer, **Michael Garvin**

Michael Garvin is a world-class songwriter, guitarist, and trumpeter, hailing from Shreveport, Louisiana. Garvin's first success came as a songwriter and is widely known to pen the global Number One hit, "Waiting for Tonight" recorded by Jennifer Lopez, and the worldwide, multi-platinum "Never Give Up on a Good Thing" for George Benson.

At 18, Michael moved to Nashville, TN, and lived his first year there as a 'starving artist' with his wife, Liv, before landing his first songwriting deal with Blake Melvis at ABC Dunhill. Michael credits Blake with not only being the first to see his potential as a songwriter but also as a lead guitarist. At the age of 19, he wrote his first Top 5 record there, "If the World Ran Out of Love Tonight," recorded by Jim Ed Brown and Helen Cornelius, also recorded by England Dan and John Ford Coley to become a Top 40 US Pop Hit. You might think it was easy sailing from there on out. "Absolutely not," Michael laughs, "It's been a roller coaster ride, but looking back, I've enjoyed every moment of the struggle, it's made me who I am."

Another defining moment for the arc of Michael's career was landing a UK publishing deal with Torquil Creevy and Miles Copeland, who's work with Sting and The Police, opened doors to Europe and the rest of the world to him. Ever since then, the world has been Michael's territory.

Working in multiple countries and genres, Garvin's MO is to bring elements from one music style to another, always keeping what he delivers fresh and exciting. It has earned him a total of 33 top ten hits so far, of which 23 hit Number One on the charts.

Garvin now brings the same hit-making skills and passion that make him a star songwriter to being an instrumental recording artist, bringing all his skills together, as a composer, a player, and a producer. He has already released four singles with significant chart activity in Smooth Jazz and Groove Jazz, including "Vibe Taxi" which was released on his first full-length album October 2018.

Do you believe drive, passion, and stamina (energy level) play a major role in helping a person to become a successful hit songwriter?

Drive, passion, and stamina play a huge role in becoming a successful songwriter because so many people want to BE professional songwriters, and so many people want to STAY professional songwriters.... You've got to put in the many, many hours making the songs as good as they can be, and the time marketing those songs, to even stand a chance...

Interview with Songwriter / Producer / Artist **Michael Garvin**

Do you think work ethic plays a vital part in becoming a hit songwriter? If so, how?

Yes, I do...You have to hit it hard, and push yourself even when you don't "feel" like it.... Especially after a painful rejection, to "get right back on the horse" ... can be extremely difficult.

How much does faith and belief in one's abilities help in becoming a hit songwriter?

It's a thin line between arrogance and confidence. In fact, it may be closer to the same thing than any of us would like to admit, but I can without a day say I never knew a songwriter who kept having hits who didn't have a little of both. Something has to make you say, "Yes I Can" when a whole lot of people are saying, "No You Can't."

How much of focus to detail and perfection helps make a hit songwriter?

I have to honestly answer that one yes and no. Yes, focusing on detail and perfection, saying, "This can be better," rewriting, and rewriting the re-write is the way to get the best result....B—U—T—It can also be what makes you never complete a song.....It's something I wrestle with a lot myself...My output would be more if I didn't second guess myself so much...

What role does commitment to short and long-term goals affect success as a hit songwriter?

I don't think "I'm gonna have my first top ten by the time I'm thirty" Etc., is healthy or realistic?... These things are beyond our control, the one thing we can control is how hard we work to utilize gifts God has given us, making our work the best it can be, and making the world aware of it....If the goal is writing the best song you can write, then YOU ARE A SUCCESSFUL SONGWRITER, in a roomful of Grammys, or a roomful of friends who love your songs.

Do you believe that learning from failures and rejections help in becoming a hit songwriter? Please elaborate.

Oh yes, I believe that learning from past failures and rejections help you (or I should say "CAN HELP YOU" in becoming a hit songwriter. I always listen to criticism. I take it in. I make a mental note of what didn't work for someone...If I start getting a lot of the same criticism, I go "Maybe they are right, let me rethink that"... Keep in mind, that something someone hates, might be the thing in a song that someone else loves...So get more than one opinion before you give up on something you believe in...

Do you feel like being obsessive and persistent with writing help in becoming a successful hit songwriter? If so, how?

Absolutely being obsessive and persistent are job requirements for being a commercially successful songwriter...it doesn't guarantee success, but without drive you don't have a chance.

Do you think taking risks in your career has helped you become successful? If so, how?

You must risk, you must risk a lot. You must gamble on devoting a lot of time and resources to a dream that may or may not become a reality, financially...My wife and I, (SHE HAD TO RISK TOO!) moved to Nashville with nothing, moved to Los Angeles, and back to Nashville, chasing a career as a songwriter....You can't wait for it to come to you. Somewhere along the way, I realized I was very successful, but truly it never felt that way because I was always chasing the next hit. So, yes, no risk....no chance of reward...Harlan Howard always said, "You have to present to win." True!

Do you believe having a positive mental attitude, being optimistic, and possessing strong self-esteem play a major role in success? If so, how?

Interview with Songwriter / Producer / Artist **Michael Garvin**

Yes, I do believe a positive mental attitude, being optimistic, and possessing a strong self-esteem play a major role in success. To do great art, you have to believe you can do great art, and to do that great art, you need to believe that art will be noticed. And I would also say that it's a great help to believe that you will be acknowledged for that art.

Of course, we all know great songs go unnoticed all the time, but we must mentally ignore that in order to write the great songs. Live in a state of mind that's not entirely the way the world is? Absolutely!
Job Requirement!

Does being a doer and not a talker help in becoming successful? If so, how?

Of course, you can't only talk about climbing the mountain; you gotta take that first step...

Does being a visionary or a dreamer help artists become successful? If so, how?

Absolutely, being a dreamer is crucial... That's what creators are...dreamers...they call us visionaries after the dreams come true...hahaha...but we've gotta dream em' first.

Do you think overall personality contributes to the success of a songwriter? If so, how?

It helps if people like you and want to be with you and work with you, and help good things happen for you, that's human nature.

Do you feel patience and practice play a role in the creation of a hit songwriter?

Patience is probably the most important asset a songwriter can have...Because when things happen is when they happen, not when you want them to....You gotta keep on writing and networking, so that when the opportunity is there (which may take years) you are ready with the right song...Be ready to wait a while to get paid for that song, by the way...hahahaha

How much prioritizing your life from day-to-day helps you become successful?

Well, you certainly have to make sure you set enough time aside to continue to perfect your craft.... what that time is varies from person-to-person.... Most of the great writers are mentally writing all the time.... they can't help it.

Do you continue to learn all you can about your profession? If so, how?

I still study other writers; listen to whatever's the hot new thing. It keeps you fresh and inspired, it's important to stay on top of what's happening on a business level too, not just a creative level.... how we are paid for instance is very different from when I started, but that's a whole other discussion...My big point to leave you with here is the more you know, the better your chances are at being able to deliver the goods...whatever that may be at the time.

In any part of your life, has self-discipline played a major role in helping become successful? If so, how?

Yes, self-discipline is very important to being a successful songwriter...I've never had to deal with self-discipline in terms of making myself work. I love to write so much; that part's been easy. What has not been so easy for me is taking care of clearances, licensing, etc....and frankly finishing songs I'm in the middle of... It's always such an orgasmic rush to start something new...that I sometimes am slow to finish what I wrote last week...I'm working on that...Thankfully, most people that know me know I will deliver the song (or the record), and it will be worth the wait...I need to be a quicker closer though, and I know it.

Interview with Songwriter / Producer / Artist **Michael Garvin**

Is there any factor, trait, or ingredient we may have omitted that helps in becoming a successful, hit songwriter?

Yes, I do...and that is if what you gravitate too naturally as a writer, is what other people naturally gravitate to as listeners, that's the singular greatest gift you can have...

Do you believe a hit songwriter is born or made? Explain your thoughts.

Interesting question, because it so relates to the last one...Talent is born, so in that sense, songwriters are born, but to grow talent into a career is something that depends on WHAT YOU DO WITH THAT TALENT, so that part of it is made. So, I'd say both.

Do you believe talent is a gift or is it earned? Explain your thoughts.

Talent is a gift from God. I don't believe you can earn it... You can only work at refining it... I don't mean for that to sound harsh, I think God gifts all of us, and some of us are gifted at other things... Life's journey is about finding out what it is we are designed to do... I believe that's where we find our bliss.

Do you believe that talent comes from within? If so, is it how they process stimuli in life?

Only in the sense that God is within. As well as without... To quote George Harrison... We may find talent within, but we didn't put it there...

What is talent?

Wow! That's a hard one to define. I'd say a preprogrammed ability to do something way beyond, the skills you could learn in a lifetime... It's a real miracle, and it's a beautiful thing to behold... Like when you look at Van Gogh's "Starry Night."

Do you believe self-criticism helps or harms the success of a hit songwriter?

Both... you've gotta be self-critical to keep working to make a song better... you've also got not to be too self-critical, or you'll never finish that song... or if you do finish it, you'll never play it for anyone... Again, you gotta have that perfect storm of both self-criticism and self-confidence.

Do you believe hit songwriters are more attuned to what is going on and happening around them than others?

Emotionally, yes for sure, we are extremely attuned to what we feel, and others around feel... that's where we draw our inspiration... In every other way, I think, most of us live outside the real world to some degree... Like right now, I'm wondering why the woman across from me at the coffee shop in Amsterdam looks so sad... and I've got all these scenarios playing out in my mind... on the other hand, I just missed my train... hahahahahaha.

Do you believe inspiration is a state of mind, and could it be a major factor in the creation of a hit songwriter? Why?

I believe being "ready to receive inspiration" is a state of mind, and is indeed a job requirement to be a hit songwriter...

Chapter Seven:

Interview with Songwriter **Jenny Slate Lee**

Hit songwriter, **Jenny Slate Lee**

Jenny Slate Lee was born and raised in Nashville, Tennessee. She ran the halls of her parent's award-winning publishing and management companies as a child. She watched as the careers of country music artists Joe Diffie, Tim McGraw, Ty Herndon, and many more were cultivated. Standing by her Dad's side as he produced chart-topping singles, she learned the process of crafting a hit song. At the tender age of seven, she taught herself to play the piano and began her own journey in writing. By 17 she signed her first publishing deal and at 18 she was off traveling the world singing in touring shows. She has appeared on the *CBS Morning Show, The Early Show, Crook and Chase, GAC, CMT, TNN*. She also worked alongside Gene Simmons for a CBS pilot about songwriters.

Jenny is one of the rare few to have received a perfect score on the hit show *"Star Search"* with Arsenio Hall. She went on to perform around the world on Celebrity and Royal Caribbean Cruise Lines in featured productions as well as her own headliner show. She did a few more national bus tours before eventually settling back in Nashville. Jenny is a sought-after studio vocalist and has recorded numerous projects for Sony, DreamWorks, CBS, Disney, and many other publishing and advertising companies.

Her latest songwriting cut, "Beautifully Broken" hit #7 on the *Billboard* night club play, broke top 20 on *Billboard's* Christian Airplay, and hit #1 on the Country Christian music charts where it remained for 8 weeks. It was the title track to the major motion film that released nation-wide in the fall of 2018 and was recorded by 4 different artists in 4 different genres. Dove Award-winning Pop artist and co-writer, Plumb, Grammy Award-winning gospel music legend, CeCe Winans, Actress and pop singer, Emily Hahn who released the Spanish pop version, and Grammy-winning country music artist John Berry - who broke a 22 year stretch for charting a single on country radio with the song.

When she isn't songwriting, she is enjoying every moment with her husband and two children. Jenny is also a worship leader with the So Loved Experience and continues to release singles year after year.

Do you believe drive, passion, and stamina (energy level) play a major role in helping a person to become a successful hit songwriter?

I do believe that drive, passion, and stamina all play a major role in helping a person to become a successful songwriter. I like to think of those things as a train constantly moving forward, and as a creative, it's your choice to get on board and go on the journey. The choice is one you make every single day. This is not an industry that pats you on the back every week, or that has a proven method for climbing the corporate ladder, there is no guaranteed paycheck. It is a dream destination that so many will never see even though they had the talent to. So, if you don't love what that journey gives to you personally every day, it will only let you down in the end., But, if you choose to create because you can't help it, and you're full of passion, and you mix that with dedication and stamina, it's a great ride, no matter what. The daily fulfillment of creating a song is worth it all to me.

Do you think work ethic plays a vital part in becoming a hit songwriter? Is so, how?

You only need to look at the math to see it. A hit song is a very rare thing these days. If you look closely behind the song at each writer, you will see hundreds and hundreds of songs that were written before the one that was eventually cut. That is dedication to the cause of creating. Showing up and writing every day, no matter what is much easier said than done. I can find a million reasons not to get in the studio and write, but discipline and routine help me overcome that resistance.

How much does faith and belief in one's abilities help in becoming a hit songwriter?

You have to believe in yourself to write. It's a very vulnerable thing to do. And especially when you are co-writing, it's hard to put yourself out there. But the more you practice this and believe in yourself, the better you become at the whole vulnerability thing; the better you become at the craft of writing.

How much of focus to detail and perfection helps make a hit songwriter?

For me, I let go of perfection in music a long time ago. I actually like the real and authentic details that tell me a song came from the heart and wasn't compromised over perfection. But as far as the attention to details—I think that is extremely important. The math of a song, the layout, and editing once it is finished to make it even better. Editing is an art in itself. There are writers that excel in this area and can take a finished song to another level by adjusting a few words or the phrasing.

What role does commitment to short and long-term goals affect success as a hit songwriter?

I set short- and long-term goals every year. They make great reference points for those days you can't focus. Sometimes, other gigs take over my schedule (gotta pay the bills), and I need a recheck of what my ultimate goal is with this music industry. I, personally, keep a planner that breaks down each goal into action steps and every morning I reflect and journal before I start the day. I find this helps keep me inspired in my writing as well.

Do you believe that learning from failures and rejections help in becoming a hit songwriter? Please elaborate.

Rejection is a huge part of this industry. It is so important to do personal growth and keep your faith in check every so often because it's a tricky thing not to let rejection tell you lies. I like to look at "nos" as shortcuts to the bigger "yesses" that lie ahead. I believe that our failures are lessons to be learned along the way. They absolutely help us to grow as artists, writers, and as people. In those times, you feel vulnerable or hurt; it helps to breathe it in and capture it for a future song one day. You can't really write about things you haven't experienced in a true, authentic way, so when you are walking through some dark times, it helps to know it's making you a stronger writer.

Do you feel like being obsessive and persistent with writing help in becoming a successful hit songwriter? If so, how?

I think as creatives we are all obsessed in some way with music. If I am not writing it, I am listening to it, or playing it, or producing it, or recording it, or collecting it, or singing it, or talking about it. Music is a constant in my life. Those who spend more time making it than talking about it are usually the ones you find on the charts.

Do you think taking risks in your career has helped you become successful? If so, how?

I am not a risk taker by nature, so I would say that the lack of taking risks in this industry has likely held me back in some regards. This is a business that is built on relationships, and the funny thing is there are so many introverts like me who are creating some great things but not doing the groundwork to get it heard because it feels too risky to network. So, for me, this is an area I am working on. Be willing to put it out there, the worst that can happen is a 'no,' which is far better than a 'what if.'

Do you believe having a positive mental attitude, being optimistic, and possessing strong self-esteem play a major role in success? If so, how?

I believe having a positive mindset is vital in life. It is incredible what shifting your focus onto gratitude can do for transformation. I believe that positive attracts positive. So, if there are dreams you have, setting a mental attitude that is humble, hungry, and positive will help you achieve them faster. This rings true for co-writes and collaborations. You may have the choice of two talented people to work with, but one has a reputation for being difficult and negative and the other positive and easy to get along with... who would you choose to work with?

Does being a doer and not a talker help in becoming successful? If so, how?

I think you have to have a little bit of both. When your co-writing you want to create an atmosphere that will help you get to the end goal, which is a hit song. So, being comfortable talking and getting each other inspired is pretty vital in the creative setting as well as getting to the work of crafting the song.

Does being a visionary or a dreamer help artists become successful? If so, how?

Having a vision is everything in this industry. There are many scriptures that talk about if there is no vision, the people perish. It is hard to stay focused on what you want if you don't know what you want. A vision for the type of artist or writer you want to evolve into helps with production, team, and in the writing process. When you are starting out, you can't focus on them all. Find your sound, what sets you apart, and go after that 100%.

Do you think overall personality contributes to the success of a songwriter? If so, how?

There seems to be a variety of personalities in the songwriting world; a beautiful blend of extroverts and introverts. Those who light up a room when they walk in, and those who have a calming nature about them. I don't think there is one personality type that rises in this business. But the work ethic behind the personality is what makes the difference.

Do you feel patience and practice play a role in the creation of a hit songwriter?

Absolutely, patience and practice play a key role in the making of a hit songwriter. In Malcolm Gladwell's "Outliers," it is said that putting in 10,000 hours of dedication and practice to something makes you a master at it. Those who don't give up and put in the work day in and day out eventually step above the rest. There are so many factors in songwriting. Listening to what's on the radio constantly. (If its radio you are writing for) Understanding the demographic you are writing for. Knowing the rising artists as well as the established ones in the genre you are in. Understanding what you excel in when in the writing room. Are you more of a melodic person, or do lyrics come more naturally? Are you a track writer? A topliner? Everyone has a different gift when it comes to songwriting and knowing your strengths will help set you up for more success. You will know who to look for that brings something different out in you. Patience is something every songwriter will struggle with as the "hurry and wait" motto is very accurate. There are times that you feel like you are riding waves, but there are more times where you are drifting in search of the next thing. That's when the discipline of how you spend your time can benefit you or hold you back. If you spend your time practicing and learning new instruments and techniques, always growing and always writing---if will pay off.

How much prioritizing your life from day-to-day helps you become successful?

I think I am touching on this answer above as well. To continue on it, there are choices we make every day that can add up. The choice to set a morning routine that gets your creativity going can set you up for a productive day. When I started doing this a few years ago, I can tell you it honestly changed my life. I felt I had so much more time in the rest of my day. And I have found writing comes more easily when I am disciplined in my routine. I love to get up early, grab my coffee and green drink, and head up to my creative space. It has a comfy seat and lots of inspiring quotes, scriptures, and artwork hanging around it. My routine has prayer, meditation, journaling, exercise, and reading in it. Then I choose what instrument to practice for 20 minutes. That way when I get to the studio later in the morning, I am feeling fully ready to write. I have cleared my head and filled my heart with things that inspire me. On the days where you feel writer's block coming on, shake up your routine and go to a movie, or read a book that you know will inspire you, or go for a hike somewhere new. I also love to write at local coffee shops with my headphones in. People watching and the sights and smells help bring creativity out.

Do you continue to learn all you can about your profession? If so, how?

Never stop growing. I love learning new things. This year alone, I enrolled in two different certification courses to learn new things about the recording studio and myself. I have also picked up a new instrument and have felt the beautiful frustration of having to start from the beginning with a dream of being good at playing it in the future. Time and patience. Daily choices. These all help us grow into better songwriters, better artists, and better people. I do think learning a DAW will help you grow as a writer. When you can build the tracks you hear in your head, it takes your writing to another level.

In any part of your life, has self-discipline played a major role in helping become successful? If so, how?

I think I have covered self-discipline in most of these questions. It's hard! But I believe it pays off in the end. A book I highly recommend is "The War of Art" by Steven Pressfield.

Is there any factor, trait, or ingredient we may have omitted that helps in becoming a successful, hit songwriter?

One thing we haven't covered is the business side of songwriting. I am constantly studying charts, insider tips on streaming and where the market is headed with that. Radio has a formula you can really start to understand when you look further into it. And the great thing about being a songwriter today is that it is anybody's guess what will happen in the next few years with the music industry. There is a beautiful change happening for songwriter rights and a unity among writers that we haven't ever seen before. Together, no matter what genre you write in, writers are making a difference. I encourage you to study the history of publishing and composers. Understanding that though you are selling something you can't hold, it is still an intellectual property you conceived and you as a writer, have rights.

Interview with Songwriter **Jenny Slate Lee**

Do you believe a hit songwriter is born or made? Explain your thoughts.

I love this question! I believe a songwriter is born AND made. I believe there are many great songwriters walking around that never gave it their best shot. They never fully committed to their passion and talents. They did not see the value in doing the work that it takes to nurture their gifts. I also believe it is never too late.

Do you believe talent is a gift or is it earned? Explain your thoughts.

I do believe talent is a gift. And no matter what our circumstances, we all seem to "pay our dues" in this industry before we earn respect. I think that is just a part of life.

What is talent?

Talent is the thing that comes naturally to you that partners with the desires and passions placed with your heart. When focus, vision, and determination meet this place, and there is a need for it in the world; that is where success is born.

Do you believe self-criticism helps or harms the success of a hit songwriter?

Self-criticism is a tough one for creatives. While there does take a certain amount of honesty and criticism to move forward and become the best you can be, there can be an imbalance here that keeps you from moving forward if you get stuck in it. Remember to keep the focus on the songs you are making, and not let it get personal. If you find you are constantly striving for something that isn't working, let go of it, and try something different.

Do you believe hit songwriters are more attuned to what is going on and happening around them than others?

I think it is important for songwriters to know what is going on around them. The music business is always changing. Keeping up can seem overwhelming, but a little research time set aside every week can help keep you in the loop without getting too caught up in it. There are so many great podcasts, articles, and interviews to look up.

Do you believe inspiration is a state of mind, and could it be a major factor in the creation of a hit songwriter? Why?

Inspiration is a state of mind. When you feel it in abundance, you tend to find writing comes more naturally. When it feels distant, the key is to not stress and strive. But to let go, change routine, do something different. Go to a museum. Go to a concert. Go to a movie. Go on vacation. Discover something new. Take a class. All these things lead you back to inspiration.

Do you believe having empathy helps in becoming a hit songwriter? Explain.

Empathy and life's experiences will and should always play a role in what you write. If you write something that you have lived through, that you are battling or that you are celebrating, that thing you can't find words to talk about but somehow you can sing about... well, that's when the formula for a hit usually brews.

Chapter Eight:

Interview with Songwriter/Producer **Michael Jay**

Hit songwriter/producer, **Michael Jay**

Michael Jay has over 30 years experience in the music business which includes a background in radio, promotion, marketing, and A&R. He also has in-studio experience as a creative talent with hit credits as a songwriter, lyricist, record producer and musician. His songs have sold more than 75 million records worldwide.

Michael Jay entered the music business as an A&R executive at Curtis Mayfield's Custom Records in Chicago. After moving to Los Angeles, he was signed as a songwriter to Famous Music, the music division of Paramount Pictures, where he instantly landed a song on the multi-platinum "Top Gun" movie soundtrack.

In the 1980s Michael Jay discovered, developed and shopped a record deal for Martika from The Disney Channel's *"Kids Incorporated"* TV show. He co-wrote and produced Martika's entire million-selling debut album including the worldwide #1 hit "Toy Soldiers." Years later, rap superstar Eminem recorded a new version of "Toy Soldiers," and it became a hit all over again.

In the 1990s Michael Jay wrote the song "Declaration of Love" which Celine Dion recorded for her Grammy Award-winning Album of The Year "Falling into You."

As a songwriter and / or producer, Michael Jay's credits include the following artists: EMINEM, CELINE DION, MANDY MOORE, KYLIE MINOGUE, GLORIA ESTEFAN. DE LA SOUL, LARA FABIAN, NEW KIDS ON THE BLOCK, JON SECADA, MELISSA MANCHESTER, PETER ALLEN, JENNIFER PAIGE, ANIMOTION, STEPHANIE MILLS, E.G. DAILY, DEBORAH HARRY, FIVE STAR, PATRICE RUSHEN, WILLA FORD, BRENDA K. STARR. EXPOSE, KRISTINIA DeBARGE, EVELYN "CHAMPAGNE" KING. LALAH HATHAWAY, GIRLS GENERATION, and many others…

Do you believe drive, passion, and stamina (energy level) play a major role in helping a person to become a successful hit songwriter?

I think everyone is born with a passion for music. But to create music, you need to be driven by a deep desire to express yourself musically. And, yes stamina is important too. You need patience because nothing happens overnight. You need to have thick skin and ignore rejection. You need to risk it all without a safety net. Having another career choice to fall back on shouldn't be an option. I always go for broke.

Do you think work ethic plays a vital part in becoming a hit songwriter? If so, how?

Well, you have to put in the hours. It's a lot of work. There's the creative part, which is fun. But then there's the networking, trying to find placements for your songs. Dealing with the business side is very demanding on your time. But you have to balance both.

How much does faith and belief in one's abilities help in becoming a hit songwriter?

Confidence is key. If you appear to be super-confident, people will pay attention.

How much of focus to detail and perfection helps make a hit songwriter?

I'm never sure if I'm being a perfectionist or just overthinking things. It often seems that my songs are always a work-in-progress. Even after they become hits, I still think of tweaks and things that might improve them.

What role does commitment to short and long-term goals affect success as a hit songwriter?

Short or long term, if you have a goal, always commit to it.

Do you believe that learning from failures and rejections help in becoming a hit songwriter? Please elaborate.

Mistakes can be great teachable moments. But how do you define a failure? I've had songs released that failed to become hits, but I still think they're great songs. There are so many other factors that go into what makes a song a hit, and we can't control them. Rejection is another matter. I don't believe in it. I know many songwriters who have rejection letters from Clive Davis for a song that eventually became a hit for an artist at another label. That's not criticism of Mr. Davis. He has the best ears in the business for hit songs, and a track record that proves it. But it shows how nobody can be right 100% of the time. A rejection is just the opinion of one person. I once had a song rejected by an A & R executive, but when I had the opportunity to play the song for the artist directly, that artist loved it, recorded it, and it made it on the album. I reject rejection.

Do you feel like being obsessive and persistent with writing help in becoming a successful hit songwriter? If so, how?

I would say I am obsessive about songwriting. Been doing it my whole life. And if I wasn't persistent, I'd still be sitting in my room, listening to other to other people's songs instead of getting my own out there.

Do you think taking risks in your career has helped you become successful? If so, how?

When I first started, every A & R person I met wanted something that sounded like another song on the radio. They always tell you to think outside of the box, but at the end of the day, they usually settle for the safe-sounding, commercial hits. When I finally had the opportunity to work with an artist for which I had a lot of creative control, I decided to experiment with a song that was a little different. That was Martika's "Toy Soldiers." Having an eerie children's choir sing in the choruses was a commercial risk that paid off. It resulted in my first #1 hit.

Do you believe having a positive mental attitude, being optimistic, and possessing strong self-esteem play a major role in success? If so, how?

I think I'm optimistic to a fault. But I couldn't go into a writing or recording session unless I had a positive attitude. Like I said before, confidence is key. And the artists and writers you're working with will feed off of your confidence.

Interview with Songwriter/Producer **Michael Jay**

Does being a doer and not a talker help in becoming successful? If so, how?

I think that question answers itself. Those who do, do. Those who talk, talk.

Does being a visionary or a dreamer help artists become successful? If so, how?

I always like to say if you can dream it, you can be it. I visualized my career when I was seven years old. I chose a path and followed it. There were bumps, detours, and U-turns, but I never let anything stop me.

Do you think overall personality contributes to the success of a songwriter? If so, how?

Well, nobody wants to work with someone who isn't fun to be around.

Do you feel patience and practice play a role in the creation of a hit songwriter?

Patience goes with stamina. You must be prepared for things to take a long time in this business. Any craft or skill requires constant practice, even songwriting. But I would also add that studying is important too. Hit songs of the past are our textbooks. You may also find them to be a great source of inspiration.

How much prioritizing your life from day-to-day helps you become successful?

There aren't enough hours in the day to work on every project that might be available to you. So, you have to learn how to prioritize the best projects for you, and how to walk away from some projects that might weigh you down.

Do you continue to learn all you can about your profession? If so, how?

The business is constantly changing. I'm always trying to keep up, follow the changes and adapt to the new ways. I'll admit, I don't understand the current trend of ten-to-twelve writers on a 3-minute song. But I've been on a few of those myself because I don't close my mind to anything.

In any part of your life, has self-discipline played a major role in helping become successful? If so, how?

In every part. If you can't discipline yourself, you risk being a loose cannon.

Is there any factor, trait, or ingredient we may have omitted that helps in becoming a successful, hit songwriter?

I think you pretty much covered it all.

Do you believe a hit songwriter is born or made? Explain your thoughts.

Natural talents usually find a way of manifesting themselves in people as they start to grow up. But I also believe skills can be learned. Not every rocket scientist is born with a gift of mathematics. Some need to study their craft.

Do you believe talent is a gift or is it earned? Explain your thoughts.

I think this would be the same answer as question 18 above.

Do you believe that talent comes from within? If so, is it how they process stimuli in life?

Sounds like a fancy way of saying that life inspires artists. I do believe in inspiration. But it's also good to be able to force yourself to be creative in times when inspiration might be absent.

Interview with Songwriter/Producer **Michael Jay**

What is talent?

The ability to do something extraordinary. I swear I didn't just look that up!

Do you believe self-criticism helps or harms the success of a hit songwriter?

I always edit myself. I think I said earlier that I consider every song a work-in-progress, sometimes even after it becomes a hit. But too much self-criticism puts you in danger of never finishing anything.

Do you believe hit songwriters are more attuned to what is going on and happening around them than others?

I think it's important for any person to stay informed; not just songwriters or artists.

Do you believe inspiration is a state of mind, and could it be a major factor in the creation of a hit songwriter? Why?

I actually liked what you said in question 20 above. Inspiration is the result of how we process stimuli in life.

Do you believe having empathy helps in becoming a hit songwriter? Explain.

Yes. People should have empathy.

LEFT: **Michael Jay** with **Celine Dion**.

ABOVE: **Michael Jay** with **Melissa Manchester.**

Chapter Nine:

Interview with Songwriter / Producer **Jud Friedman**

Hit songwriter, producer, and music business attorney, **Jud Friedman**

His family still claims he sang and played music before he talked. Well, who knows...but it's a great story for holiday dinners. But for sure the music has always been in him. Jud Friedman grew up in New York and Connecticut and went to Yale and Harvard Law School (long story...), all the while playing in various bands, performing in musical theater and writing songs. After headlining a show in New York City, Jud had an epiphany – he loved performing, but didn't crave it or the limelight the way he thought he needed to if he wanted to be a star. What he really craved was...to make music. And Jud realized he could do it for other people.

So, Jud moved to Los Angeles and started honing his writing and producing craft. After several years, he had his first Number One hit as a writer and arranger: "I Don't Have the Heart" by James Ingram. And the ball was rolling. Next, Whitney Houston recorded "Run to You" for her film "The Bodyguard." Jud made the record with David Foster, worked on producing Whitney's vocals and even sang backgrounds with her. "Run to You" was nominated for an Oscar and a Grammy. Then Jud wrote "For the First Time" for the film "One Fine Day" with Michelle Pfeiffer and George Clooney. Kenny Loggins performed it and the song garnered another Oscar and Grammy and a Golden Globe nomination.

Along the way, there were lots more hits and nominations, with amazing artists such as Barbra Streisand, Ray Charles, Tina Turner, Rod Stewart, Leann Rimes, Chaka Khan, Kristine W., Oleta Adams, Gladys Knight, and Dave Koz. And recently, big records with Charice ("The Truth Is"), Toni Braxton ("If I Have to Wait") and Kimberley Locke of American Idol fame, number one singles on the number one CDs of Italian divas Giorgia and Elisa, and songs recorded by massive pop/classical group The Tenors on their Juno-winning CD, Right Said Fred and many more. Also, a couple of things for television: the theme song from the Michael Jackson show "Man In The Mirror" ("Believe In Me") and the score for the TV film "The Prince and The Pizza Boy," starring Joey Lawrence. (One of Jud's biggest TV successes; He still gets mobbed by little kids on the street. Ha-ha.)

Jud Friedman has 65 million records sold worldwide. At last count, Jud has had nominations for 2 Academy Awards, 2 Grammys, 2 Golden Globes and, for artists singing his songs, nominations for two more Grammys and a Soul Train Award.

In March 2016 the Grammy Museum did a special night celebrating the more than 25-year career of Jud's long-term songwriting partner Allan Rich and himself.

Interview with Songwriter / Producer **Jud Friedman**

Do you believe drive, passion, and stamina (energy level) play a major role in helping a person to become a successful hit songwriter?

Of course, absolutely. The entertainment business in general including songwriting is if not the most competitive business in the world, certainly right up there. So to become a hit writer, it is very, very important to have a lot of passion and ambition. If you're not driven to do this stuff, there's no way it will happen. Even if you are Beethoven, Stevie Wonder or Mozart sitting in your room cranking out brilliant music, no one's going to find you. You've got to be able to get out there and pound the pavements; in fact, more so than ever. When I was coming up as a songwriter, there was still a little bit of a dichotomy between the songwriter who would do the creative stuff and his/her representatives who would do the business stuff. Now you almost have to be the all-in-one, do-everything-yourself person. You're expected to write the songs, demo them, promote them, create the brand for the song and yourself, do extensive social media, get on Spotify—it's endless. Can we stop now? I'm exhausted.

Do you think work ethic plays a vital part in becoming a hit songwriter? Is so, how?

Absolutely. Same answer. And by the way, everybody's work ethic is different - whatever works...pardon the pun. For me, songwriting and record producing have never been a regularly scheduled job, as in I will get up at a certain time, I will write for a certain number of hours, I will take a break, I will have a chocolate bar. It's never been like that for me, but it's a constant pursuit. You can't wait around for inspiration or for someone to approach you with a business opportunity. It's work, work, work a lot of the time. But you need to give yourself some downtime to live your life, so you have things to write about. We're human beings first. Spend time with your family.

How much does faith and belief in one's abilities help in becoming a hit songwriter? If so, how?

I can't speak for everyone, but I think faith in your abilities is critical in every pursuit in life. And again, succeeding as a writer is such a daunting task. If you're looking up at that mountain and thinking about how hard it will be to climb, and you don't believe 1000 percent in yourself, there's no way you'll be able to take even that first step, let alone the second, third... It's hard and stressful enough, even when you do believe in yourself. It's a "no" business, no matter how successful you are. Everyone's going to say "no" and "you stink," basically, although if they're nice maybe not in those exact words. I have an expression that "opinions are like assholes; everyone's got one." If you don't really believe in yourself, there's no way. It's not going to happen.

How much of focus to detail and perfection helps make a hit songwriter?

You know I teach songwriting and we talk about this a lot. I don't believe in "perfection." I am much more a big picture, "forest" vs. "trees" person. The way I experience life and music is not to focus on every detail. What did that word in the 11th verse mean? Shouldn't that have been a semi-colon and not a comma in the 27th chorus? You listen to a song on the radio and it either washes over you and makes you feel something, moves you, makes you want to dance or cry or laugh or makes you want to turn it off. But you're not listening note by note, word by word, comma by comma. In fact, when you go back and look at the lyrics to some of the most successful songs - and I do this all the time with my students, it's an interesting phenomenon - in the vast majority of cases, I'm telling you at least 70 to 80 percent of those lyrics are, for the most part, unintelligible. Forget about rhymes, read the lyrics. And you'll go "what the hell?" But, there's something in that song, some vibe, some overall message that comes through, one line in the chorus, one transcendent hook where the message is totally clear, and it just hits you. It can be "feel," it can be one phrase or melody; it can be one instrumental hook. Something about the song just works for you even if all the details aren't right. I remember an interview with Steven Spielberg about the making of "Raiders of the Lost Ark." He was talking about watching a late cut of the movie and seeing a million little issues. He said something like "I knew we could go back and spend a couple more weeks and another 10 million dollars fixing all those little things, but you know what - the movie worked. It made me feel something; I liked it. It felt great. So, I just decided to stop tweaking and put it out the way it was." And you know, that film did alright. I think detail and the quest for so-called perfection can be the enemy of great work and success. You get too caught up in "we've got to work four more hours on the snare drum sound." Nobody cares about that. You've got to let it go at some point.

What role does commitment to short and long-term goals affect success as a hit songwriter?

Everybody's method to inspire themselves is different. I make a million to-do lists. But I don't usually think of my goals for next month, or the year, or the next five years. If that works for you, great. I think when you're first starting out, to a certain extent you have to ignore the realities. You can't really think of in terms of "I should be here in a year," because you'll be disappointed. You can't stare up at the top of the mountain. You just have to put blinders on and go forward one step at a time without thinking about how hard it really is. To me, it may actually be self-defeating to make a list of where you want to be and when because it is almost inevitable that you won't be there then. You just have to keep making amazing music the best you can and get better and better. Keep your eyes open; keep pushing forward in all the areas you need to push forward in. But for me, timetables and specific timelines and goals have never been a part of the process.

Do you believe that learning from failures and rejections help in becoming a hit songwriter? Please elaborate.

Well first off what is failure? Again, opinions are like assholes; everyone's got one. People's opinions of music are completely subjective. So, you have to balance between "everyone's saying this song isn't hitting them, so maybe I didn't quite nail this one" with that thing we talked about a few minutes ago, that total faith and confidence in yourself and the confidence to be able to say "you know what, to hell with those guys, I think it's great." So, yes, failure can be very healthy to the extent that you actually think "You know what, they are right, I can do better. I'm accepting that. I think I should try to work on those things and learn from this experience." But also, you have to learn who to trust when it comes to accepting the concept of failure. As I said before, everyone's going to say no. You have to pick and choose your mentors along the way. You need to know who you can play a song for because you can really respect their response and know that it is coming from a place of love and support as opposed to being some random or knee jerk "no." I tell my students all the time, "Hey, I'm only here to make you great songwriters. I have no ego in this thing. So, anything I have to say, I have a circular ideas file also known as a garbage can in my studio. Imagine it sitting here. Anything I say that doesn't work for you, throw it in there. But if as your teacher I suggest to you, not that you're failing, but that maybe this song could be better, at least think about it because I'm someone you can trust - I'm here to help." And in terms of rejection - since it will happen the vast majority of times when you knock on a music business door, you've got to be able to take it. If you're person who can't accept rejection - "I pitched the song, they didn't take it, or they didn't like it" - and literally go, "That stinks, what a drag" for about 30 seconds and then forget about it and move on to the next thing, you shouldn't be a songwriter. Because you are going to be bombarded with rejection. If you can't accept that, don't do it.

Interview with Songwriter / Producer **Jud Friedman**

Do you feel like being obsessive and persistent with writing help in becoming a successful hit songwriter? If so, how?

I don't think obsessive is ever healthy; I'm not a big fan. If it works for you, great. To me, you have to have a balance in your life. From my experience, the vast majority of obsessive people are not happy and get burnt out. One huge exception is Diane Warren, who lives, breathes and sleeps music. I love Diane. She's a wonderful person and an incredible songwriter. But for me at least, I think it's better to work smarter, not harder. Focus. Be efficient. Don't hang out in the studio partying for four hours and then say, Let's write the song." Spend the four hours actually working. Don't be on your cell phone. Put your blinders on. Take everything else out of the picture. But don't be obsessive. Live a balanced life.

Do you think taking risks in your career has helped you become successful? If so, how?

By definition, being a songwriter is incredibly risky. There are certain jobs, certain pursuits in life where the path is fairly well trod, and you know what you're getting. There may be a definite ceiling to the job, but it pays the bills, and you're okay with it. Maybe it's not going to thrill you, but you've got other things you like to do that fill up your life. And that is perfectly fine. Trying to succeed in something as competitive as the music business is in itself an enormous risk. The odds are horribly against you no matter how good you are. There are so many talented people out there. It takes a very specific combination of great talent, personality, relationship skills, and work ethic as well as some luck and timing. I come across great writers all the time, and unfortunately, no one's ever going to hear many of their songs. There's just too much supply and not enough demand. So, if you're not a risk taker, forget about trying to be a pro-songwriter.

Do you believe having a positive mental attitude, being optimistic, and possessing strong self-esteem play a major role in success? If so, how?

Absolutely, in everything in life. It's seeing the glass half-full as opposed to half-empty even when you're banging your head against the wall with frustration. As a songwriter, you have the absolute right to be pissed and hate the music business - jeez that's like an everyday thing for me! - But if that takes you over you won't be productive and more importantly, you'll be bitter and unhappy. It's always supposed to be fun; you have to enjoy the process. My co-writing partner and great buddy Allan Rich tells this story about a song he was writing with Barry Manilow. When they were finished, Barry turned to him and said, "Allan, do you know how excited we are about this song right now? Enjoy this moment. It's never going to be this pure again. Everybody's going to start picking the song apart and saying how terrible it is." The process of making the music, being in the room with creative people, watching sparks fly while you're eating—the whole journey of writing songs and recording them is so much fun, if you're into it. And you've got to be grateful for that experience and never take it for granted.

Does being a doer and not a talker help in becoming successful? If so, how?

I know so many people who call themselves writers, but never write anything. They're afraid to fail, or they had that one rejection, and it is too daunting to them to start something new. I'm all about doing and not talking. Just do it.

Does being a visionary or a dreamer help artists/songwriters become successful? If so, how?

A visionary, to me, is different than a dreamer. A visionary to me is a Martin Luther King or a Mozart, or Lennon and McCartney, or Einstein, or Steely Dan, who probably wouldn't even consider themselves visionaries. These are people who are on a different level, thinking in ways and creating something that no one has ever done. They're setting the bar. I think the vast majority of us, even if we feel good about ourselves and our talent, are trying to come up with new ideas in a much smaller way. Sure, we're always trying to be fresh and unique. But we're not reinventing the wheel, like true visionaries. On the other side of the coin, if you're not a dreamer, there's no way you can succeed because it is a dream every time you write a song! And success itself is a HUGE dream. Again, it's like Mount Everest. If you look up there and you can't suspend disbelief, can't ignore realities; you're going to be paralyzed. You have to think "I'm going to dream myself up this enormous mountain."

Do you think overall personality contributes to the success of a songwriter? If so, how?

When you're talking about making music and navigating the music business, in general, you are talking about relationships. If you're a jerk, no one will want to work with you, and forget about getting the best out of people. It's self-defeating on both business and creative levels. Be nice, be respectful. Be professional. Leave your ego at the door. Be open to other ideas. Don't be the jerk who is always taking over the writing session or rolling his eyes at everyone else's suggestions. And even if you stumble across someone who isn't being very nice, sometimes you just have to bite your tongue and do the best you can. And maybe try to steer clear of that person in the future. Life's too short.

Do you feel patience and practice play a role in the creation of a hit songwriter?

Well, I'm an impatient person. "Hey, I sent the email out five minutes ago; why aren't they responding??" But I've had to learn to slow things down. You know what, shockingly enough, everyone has other things to deal with besides me. Everyone is busy. I might be somewhere in the top 1000 of their priorities but not even close to their top 10. So, I try to be professional, hang back, be nice and not pushy. And you've also got to have patience as a creative person. If you're banging your head against the wall trying to nail a lyric and you're not getting anywhere, take a break. And don't fool yourself because of impatience or the psychological need we all have to feel like "we're getting somewhere." For example, when you're collaborating with someone, especially someone new, there's always this self-imposed pressure to come up with something, to justify the time you're spending. So, someone throws out an idea that maybe isn't that great - "Say, why don't we write a song about pants?" And everyone else goes "Yeah, that's brilliant; let's do it!" The next day in the cold light of reason you listen to the work tape, and you're like, "What the hell?? Why did we write that?" or maybe "It's an okay song, but not great." Take your time. Sometimes the great ones don't come to you right away. As for practice: it doesn't make perfect, but of course, it's important in every area of life. If you want to be a pro athlete, live in the gym. If you want to succeed as a writer, keep writing, keep working at getting better.

How much prioritizing your life from day-to-day helps you become successful?

Time management is really, really important, especially in this digital era. There's so much stuff on your phone; it never stops beeping with calls, texts, emails, etc. You could spend eternity responding to everyone. FedEx is knocking at the door. The gardener is here, and the air blower is driving you crazy. At a certain point you have to put blinders on and say, "Here's what I want to accomplish today; here are my priorities." We were talking before about long-term goals, which I'm not particularly into. But day-to-day goals and priorities, yeah, big time.

Do you continue to learn all you can about your profession? If so, how?

Yes, in any industry it's very valuable to keep studying and learning and to stay in touch with what's contemporary. I'm teaching now, both songwriting and music business and law. I have a law degree from Harvard. I learn a lot by thinking about what I want to tell my students about what I think their goals and approaches should be and what it takes to become a professional songwriter and write great songs. I learn probably more than they learn. Also, as preparation for the classes, I read a lot of articles about songwriting and the music business. I regularly check out the top 30 songs in the Hot 100 at Billboard.com. It's simple. Look at the songs. Why are they hits? How did they end up on the charts? Look at how many songwriters there are and the structure of the songs. Are they conventionally or strangely structured? Do they have hooks and what kind - vocal? Instrumental? Are they more "song songs" with lyrics and melodies and changes or production and track oriented songs? That kind of analysis tells you a lot about songs, songwriting and where the music business is going.

In any part of your life, has self-discipline played a major role in helping become successful? If so, how?

Yes, it plays a big part. See above!

Is there any factor, trait, or ingredient we may have omitted that helps in becoming a successful, hit songwriter?

Well as in any walk of life it's not just nurture, it's nature too. Some people say you can't teach songwriting; you have to be "born" a songwriter. To me, that isn't exactly accurate. I think you can learn a lot about songwriting; that's why I teach it. But of course, nature plays a part. I have worked very, very hard at my writing. But I was given a gift. From the time I was very little, I was playing and singing and writing my little songs. You can't teach talent. I could spend 40,000 hours practicing basketball, and I still wouldn't be LeBron James. I'm a decent athlete. But he's superhuman. He's on a different level. He was born to be a basketball player...he's killed himself to get better but he had a gift to start with. I think songwriters have to have that talent as a foundational element. If you don't, you can work very, very hard and become a very good craftsman, but maybe not a hit writer. You need to be inspired as well.

Do you believe a hit songwriter is born or made? Explain your thoughts.

Same as above, one more example of so many I could name: The Beatles. I was lucky enough to hear George Martin tell stories about when he started working with them. He would suggest X change, and they would do X, Y, and the rest of the alphabet and take it to the next level. It was a gift. They had that - and then they went and worked their asses off to get better and better. Talent and hard work: one is a precondition, and the other is a necessary following condition.

Do you believe talent is a gift or is it earned? Explain your thoughts.

More same as above. :) To me, talent by definition is a gift. I was very fortunate to have two parents both of whom were very musical, especially my dad, who was a great songwriter and musician. Thanks, Mom and Dad, I love you.

Do you believe that talent comes from within? If so, is it how they process stimuli in life?

I believe it does come from within. And over time people come to realize they are talented. Sometimes that's not a great thing if it makes you arrogant or dismissive of others, and you feel like you don't need or can't benefit from anyone else's help...or you feel like you're so good you don't need to grow. You can always grow and should always want to!

What is talent?

I think it's the obvious: something you are born with that gives you the potential to excel in whatever area or areas. Something given to you in your genes, in your persona. You still have to work at it. But again, I don't agree with the idea that anyone can become a savant in any area with 10,000 hours of practice. You got to have some talent to start with.

Do you believe self-criticism helps or harms the success of a hit songwriter?

It both helps and hurts. You have to be able to step outside of yourself a bit and critique yourself, ask yourself how you and your music can get better. But sometimes you can be too self-critical, and that's self-defeating and paralyzing.

Do you believe hit songwriters are more attuned to what is going on and happening around them than others?

I don't know. Maybe creative people, in general, tend to be a little more sensitive than others. But then again, there are all kinds of songwriters. There are some who could care less about the feelings or emotions of the songs. Allan and I tend to write songs that are more emotional.

Do you believe inspiration is a state of mind, and could it be a major factor in the creation of a hit songwriter? Why?

Inspiration is a mystery. I mean, how do you get inspired? It goes back to talent, and to the luck of the draw that you have that you maybe you feel and experience things in a deep way. That you are able to express feelings and experiences in ways that people without that talent are not able to do. I think if you are sensitive and open to it, inspiration is all around you. On the other hand, there are people who want to romanticize inspiration, "Oh my gosh it came through me, it just hit me." As a professional writer, you can't just sit around and wait for inspiration to hit you. If you're going to be a professional writer, you've got to be able to find inspiration on a regular basis. You have to find ways to put yourself in a place and state of being where you're open to being inspired and finding inspiration. In some of my classes, I suggest that the students take 10 minutes a day and write free-form, meaning write down or record whatever comes to their minds. Don't think about it. Just let it come to you. Hopefully, you'll stumble across one of those great, inspired moments and you can build a great song from it.

Do you believe having empathy helps in becoming a hit songwriter? Explain.

I am very aware of what people are feeling, and I try to be as empathetic and nurturing as possible. Empathy to me is being able to understand, feel and identify with what other people are going through, even if it's not something you think makes total sense. And I do think empathy and being able to get yourself out of your own head and out of your own perspective are critical things in songwriting. Any time you write, you're going to be writing your own story because you are always going to be yourself. You're always going to write from your own point of view. But many new songwriters try to make everything literal and base everything on their actual experiences. I'll ask my student "What does this line mean?" and she'll answer, "That's something that happened to me. It's private. It's true to the story, so I included it in the song." I'll say, "As I'm driving down the freeway listening to your song on the radio, I don't know the back story, and I don't care about it. Your job isn't to write an essay about exactly what happened two days ago. Your job is to be inspired by that event and decide what emotions you want to communicate about it." Your goal as a writer is to touch people. And do to that you have to be able to empathize with what they feel, what they go through in their lives...not just what you feel or go through. The question isn't, am I telling a true story? It's: am I communicating something universal and true?

Chapter Ten:

Interview with Songwriter / Producer **Ted Perlman**

Hit songwriter and producer, **Ted Perlman**

Ted has produced, played guitar, arranged, recorded, & toured with major artists Whitney Houston, Harry Belafonte, Bob Dylan, Diana Ross, Burt Bacharach, Christian music stars Colton Dixon & Nicole C. Mullen, Ronald Isley, Mexican pop star Alessandra Rosaldo, The Manhattans, jazz muti-Grammy winners the Manhattan Transfer, gospel legend Edwin Hawkins, Beatles drummer Ringo, Jazz legend George Duke, Joe Cocker, iconic group "Chicago", rapper Young M.C., R&B stars Howard Hewett-Deniece Williams-Stephanie Mills-Kashif-Melba Moore, father of punk music Jonathan Richman, country stars Garth Brooks & Dolly Parton, Latin music stars Willie Colon & Hector Lavoe, Phantom of the Opera star Michael Crawford, *Rolling Stone* guitarist Ron Wood, Filipino star Imelda Papin, Dr. Buzzard's Savannah Band, & pop legend Engelbert Humperdink.

All this has made Ted proficient in a variety of musical styles - R&B, Rock, Gospel, Hip-Hop, Soul, Classical, Pop, Latin, Rap, Country, World, etc. While living in Israel in the early 1970's, he worked in the studios and in concerts with top stars in that country. Ted even worked on a recording with recently deceased Israeli Prime Minister Shimon Peres. Originally from Brooklyn, New York, he now resides and works in Los Angeles.

He has done extensive work in TV & Movies. He arranged, programmed, & recorded 3 songs in the Adam Sandler movie "I Now Pronounce You Chuck And Larry," ft. Lance Bass of *NSYNC. Ted produced the song "Before We Say Goodbye" for MTV's "2gether", produced, played, & composed the score for ABC-TV's "World Stunt Awards", co-wrote the main theme & cues for Showtime's "Full Frontal Comedy" (winner of Cable ACE award for Best Stand Up Comedy), co-produced 2 songs in the Ellen Burstyn film "Walking Across Egypt", & produced the title song for Jean-Claude Van Damme's film "Desert Heat." Ted produced and co-wrote two songs for Alessandra Rosaldo, "Por Tu Amor" & "Eres," which were the title song and closing theme for the Mexican TV novella "Ni Contigo."

Ted has conducted, played guitar, & arranged music for NBC, CBS, ABC, Fox, Showtime & others. He has done jingles for McDonald's, Applebee's, Burger King, Korean Airlines, Perrier, & Coca-Cola.

He is a Pro endorser/consultant featured in ads by major companies Celemony, MAGIX, Steinberg, PSP, ADK microphones, Rob Papen, & many others. He has written for music magazines including "Computer Music" & was the subject of the first podcast by "Electronic Musician." Celemony & Trident Speakers have both filmed interviews with Ted at his studio.

Recent projects are producing the album "Alessandra" by Mexican superstar Alessandra Rosaldo), the last song The Manhattan Transfer recorded with group founder Tim Hauser, rock superstar Dave Mason of "Traffic's "26 Letters, 12 Notes", the "God's Gardeners" CD by internationally famed author Margaret Atwood, country singer Tesa James (relative of famed outlaw Jesse James), A*TEENS star Sara Lumholdt, pop legend Neil Sedaka's latest release (featuring producers David Foster & Ted), Bob Geldoff vocalist Zara Phillips, "Gospel Record & Song Of The Year" Unity Award-winning Catholic artist ValLimar Jansen, the new solo CD from longtime Manhattan Transfer member Alan Paul, & solo recordings by "Jersey Boys" Tony winner John Lloyd Young. He programmed, arranged, & recorded the top-five platinum selling UK singles "Paradise" and "I Think I Love You" for Curb Records' singer Kaci. He produced & wrote the #1 European charting CD "Livin' On Love" for American Idol's "Vocal Coach From Hell" Peggi Blu. He also worked on an arrangement of "Amazing Grace" for Lalo Schifrin and the Vienna Symphony, featuring vocal soloists Placido Domingo, Jose Carreras, and Diana Ross. Collabro, the British vocal group that won "Britain's Got Talent" were in Ted's studio recording new vocal tracks with him.

Ted won a Grammy for his work on "At This Time" by Burt Bacharach & co-produced with Burt a song on Ronald Isley's Dreamworks CD "Here I Am." On "New Music from An Old Friend," Ted played the guitar solo on Brian Wilson's "What Love Can Do" & co-produced "Still Remember" with Burt Bacharach. He mixed "The 5 Browns" duet w/Dean Martin of "Everybody Loves Somebody" (which went to #1 on *Billboard's* Classical Music charts).

Ted is especially proud of playing the two guitar solos on Bob Dylan's "Tight Connection to My Heart" from his CBS/Sony album "Empire Burlesque."

Ted is currently in production with actress/singer Gloria Loring (Robin Thicke's mom) on her new CD, featuring songs by Desmond Child, Burt Bacharach, and Robin. Robin sang backgrounds on one of them as well.

Ted is also FINALLY working on his own CD, which he intends to be a Christian-themed one. Currently, he is a member of the worship team at First Baptist Church of Pasadena. Previously he was on the worship teams at "The Crystal Cathedral" with Dr. Robert Schuller, and at First AME Church with Pastor Cecil "Chip" Murray.

In addition to his music productions, Ted has been auditing classes at Fuller Seminary, one of the most respected Theological schools in the world and studying Scientology self-improvement at Celebrity Center in Hollywood. He gives all glory to God.

Do you believe drive, passion, and stamina (energy level) play a major role in helping a person to become a successful hit songwriter?

In any successful songwriting combination, you have to have someone who is highly motivated. I used to write in groups of fives: two people who would do the lyrics, two who would do the music, and one person whose main job, after the song was done, was to push the music. Everybody should balance out. One person writes the music, one person the lyrics, but as far as the business part which is really important, if neither person has a business sense, you need to write with the third person who may contribute parts of the music, parts of the words, but they are more business savvy as far promoting the music, promoting the songs with music supervisors; otherwise it's a dead end.

Do you think work ethic plays a vital part in becoming a hit songwriter? If so, how?

Norman Gimbel just died. And I worked with Norman a lot. Norman was a big hit songwriter in all genres from TV to records, everything. He wrote, "Killing Me Softly." And I brought him to write the English lyrics on a Filipino artist which was originally written *in Tagalog. Norman called the song, 'Contradiction." We go to his house in Montecito near Santa Barbara. So, everything's great. We drive there. Norman doesn't bring anyone to his house, but because of my relationship with him, he let me bring her by. And right in the middle of "hi, how are you?", she says, "you know the title sounds a little harsh for the song." And Norman looks at me, "are you kidding me?" So, he says, "I wrote "Killing Me Softly," and they tried to make me change the word 'killing' because they said it was too harsh for a love song." But at that point, he said, "that's what I wrote, that's it." But he had the confidence, success, and the clout to say, "that's it, I'm not changing it." I work with so many hit songwriters. Hal David wrote a song with Kenny Hirsch. The first song they wrote together, Kenny wrote the melody and gives it to Hal. Hal gives it back and calls it, "Arnold Schwarzenegger." And Kenny comes before Hal. And he's sitting in the studio, almost ready to cry because of his idol, Burt Bacharach. So, he wanted to write with Hal David and finally gets to. "Look at this piece of s***. What am I going to do with this?" It was written with Hal David. But we looked at it. It became a hit for Westlife in the U.K. because in the chorus it read, "Arnold Schwarzenegger is in all your dreams at night, And Arnold Schwarzenegger wants to kiss you and hold you tight. But he couldn't begin to love you like I do." It was a great song. But when you looked at it, you thought this is a stupid song. But it wasn't because the writers had a great work ethic and had put in the hard work. Most successful hit songwriters have an incredible work ethic.*

How much does faith and belief in one's abilities help in becoming a hit songwriter?

Faith comes from a higher source. Even the songwriters I know who don't consider themselves overtly religious attribute their creative gems to a higher power because what happens is; you have a hit song, and you then have no idea why that was a hit song and all your other 50 songs your thought were great are not hit songs. Ron Dante told me when Jeff Barry and Andy Kim wrote, "Sugar, Sugar" in five minutes waiting for the studio to finish; they were running late. So, they said, "we've got some time, fifteen minutes, let's write something!" And that song will probably outlast all of us alive right now.

With the creative part to be successful, you must start with a blank page and have no attitudes. If you have any attitudes like, "I'm confident in myself because I had a hit record." But as we all know, just because you had a hit record last year doesn't mean you'll have one this year. I wrote with Arthur Hamilton who wrote, "Cry Me A River" when he was 19 and he never had another hit. I wrote with Jeff Silbar who wrote, "Wind Beneath My Wings" and later we wrote a bunch of songs. They were okay but not hits. I think in the selling part, you have to have confidence in yourself whether it's false or not to say, "I've got a great song." Marti Sharon was the best song plugger I have ever met. Because when we'd be working on a song, as soon as we got to the chorus, she would call Richard Perry or another producer, and she'd put the speaker up to the phone, and she would play it just enough to where he'd say, "oh that's really cool." She'd say, "isn't that great?" He'd say, "fantastic." She had already sold the song. She would hype the song. She would dress, talk, whatever she had to do. She had no self-confidence, but she could fake it on phone calls. She was so confident in her ability that she didn't care if she only wrote one word in a song she'd written with others. She just knew she could sell. But you've got to write with someone like that. You've got to bite the bullet, shake hands with the devil and go for it. Otherwise, the "Devil Went Down to Georgia" would have never been heard if somebody hadn't pushed Charlie Daniels.

How much of focus to detail and perfection helps make a hit songwriter?

That's a fine line. L. Ron Hubbard has a book called, "Art" which is good. In his book, he talks about perfection. He totally discusses about perfection versus communication. He says that in art sometimes people work on it to make it so perfect and it doesn't communicate to the audience. There's a point you have to say, "people like it, and maybe it's not perfect." But going for perfection over communication is the wrong way to go.

I think everything out there is imperfect. I hear songs I say, "I wish I had changed this or that." Sometimes God gives you inspiration. Take it. Don't second guess it because it's special.

What role does commitment to short and long-term goals affect success as a hit songwriter?

Commitment could also be called madness. How many people do you know that were committed to something they weren't any good at? ...and they just have this dream... Like kids you see on talent shows. They dream about being a singer and they can't sing. William Hung of "American Idol," the first season Simon Cowell comes on and says, "Are you kidding me? You can't sing at all." He says, "oh, but I believe in myself." He ended up being on the radio which was hilarious. But his belief in himself superseded his ability. You have to careful and realistic. When I first played guitar, I believed I could play and began to play instantly. But I knew I couldn't sing. So, some people said, "if you work at it, you'll get there." So, I'd work at it so I'd get to a point where the person I was working with would understand me. But I could never get it to a point where people would say, "wow, I love that person's voice." Tom Waits throws that rule out the window. People loved his voice. Was it perfect? No. But a lot of people love hearing him sing.

Do you believe that learning from failures and rejections help in becoming a hit songwriter? Please elaborate.

Okay, I'll take two things from the Bible. The book *of Ecclesiastes says, "The race isn't given to the swiftest nor to the strong." Then in the book of Matthew it says, "he who endures is saved." So, I put those together, "The race isn't given to the swiftest nor the strongest but to he who endureth to the end. Okay, if you can't take failure, you're in the wrong business no matter what you do. Michael Jordan shoots 50 shots, none of them go in, but in his mind, he can make the 51st shot. Kobe Bryant, the same way. The songwriter who keeps writing songs, no one likes that song, but he'll keep going. When we came to California, we were signed with Capitol Records, a million-dollar deal. My wife and I made an agreement that if we sell one song, we stay in California. We wrote every day and everything we turned in was, "no, no, no." Finally, we turned in a song called, "All and All." They took it and it made the album. I am here in California; otherwise, I'd be in New York talking to you.*

Do you feel like being obsessive and persistent with writing help in becoming a successful hit songwriter? If so, how?

I'd say you have to be obsessive with the whole process: obsessed with getting somebody to write with you, obsessed with writing, obsessed with trying to make it great, and obsessed with knowing when it's done. Obsession is another word for passion. Obsession has a negative overtone; passion has a positive overtone. But they're basically the same thing: commitment, obsession, passion, belief—all of them, different words for the same thing...I need to write; I need to breathe...you know for a songwriter, whether it's a hit songwriter or a songwriter who hasn't had a hit yet, the commitment to writing is as powerful as the commitment to waking up and living.

Do you think taking risks in your career has helped you become successful? If so, how?

It's risky being a songwriter, it's risky being a musician, anything in the arts. My sister is a photographer, and there's no guarantee that you're going to be successful whether you're a hit photographer, or a hit writer. I co-produced with Orville Stoeber the CD that accompanied Margaret Atwood's book, "Year of the Flood." Did she think she was going to be a hit writer? She just wrote. She has a series online, and she says you've just got to be committed to writing. That's it, whether it's a book, a song, a play...you're selling your screenplay, you're committed. Barack Obama was committed to a vision in his mind to helping people. Whatever your politics are, I try to find something positive in everybody. Donald Trump was committed to being president. My father loves Donald Trump. But I can find this one thing to talk with him that we agree on—Donald Trump believed in the face of everyone telling him you can't do that. No, you can't do that, whether it's in real estate or being on his own, people told him he couldn't do this or that. He said, "I'll show you." The "I'll show you" commitment whether it's in song, music playing.... I mean most people start out, you know, they're not very good. They work at it, and they get better. If you don't get better, maybe you ought to think about doing something else. Now, if you're writing...remember the movie, "Ishtar"? My friend, Paul Williams, wrote all the songs. Warren Beatty and Dustin Hoffman were these two guys who believed in themselves, and they were terrible. They thought they could write; they thought they could sing. They were so excited about each other, and they enabled each other's lack of talent. What did they get out of it? They really enjoyed each other's friendship. They didn't get a hit song, but they got great fellowship. Sometimes, that's just as important as writing a hit song.

Do you believe having a positive mental attitude, being optimistic, and possessing strong self-esteem play a major role in success? If so, how?

If success is helped out by the people, you're working with feeling good about working with you. There's nothing like working with an energy vampire. How are you going to write with somebody, "good morning, I can't wait to see what we come up with today." "Oh, yeah, we probably won't come up with anything because I'm not very good. I don't usually do good work on Tuesday. Everything's rotten in my life. And I don't even know why I open my eyes." The affinity part, what people say about Scientology. What I get out of it is affinity and establishing communication with people; those are good goals for anyone in the arts. David Pomeranz told me about it. Those are the skills lacking in me. So, anyone having trouble in those areas, they might want to look into some of those basic courses—self-improvement.

Does being a doer and not a talker help in becoming successful? If so, how?

Doer is more important than talker. But talking with nothing behind it, basically you should be a used car salesman. You shouldn't be in the music business.

Does being a visionary or a dreamer help artists become successful? If so, how?

You need to be a dreamer to create. Daydreaming is the most positive thing ever. I'd use take a shower for 15 minutes when we were doing an arrangement for a song that day, and they'd be knocking on my door, "what are you doing in there?" I'd hear the verse and the chorus, and I'd be arranging in my head. Daydreaming is good as long as you don't daydream while you're driving. Vision means trying something new, being not afraid to try something new.

Do you think overall personality contributes to the success of a songwriter? If so, how?

Yes.

Do you feel patience and practice play a role in the creation of a hit songwriter?

Patience is probably the thing that is in least supply of every person I know. People say, "how long is it going to take?" I'm starting from scratch, so it could take 20 minutes, it could take 10 minutes, or it could take two hours because I don't know where I'm starting from. Cause if there's nothing there, you have to work at it. I just saw something from Bruce Sweetman. He said they mixed Michael Jackson's "Billie Jean" 91 times. Michael was very nice. He would say, "Could we just try one more?" And Quincy Jones came into the studio, and asked, "are you guys done?" And they said, "we're still working." Quincy replied, "what are you guys doing?" They said, "we're mixing." Quincy said, "what" after 91 mixes. He asked, "let me hear where you are." He said, "let me hear mix number two." Quincy said, "that's the one." And that's the one that went out. They were obsessive and perfectionistic. They were chasing after something; they didn't know what it was. There's no set way to get it done in writing, producing, recording, mixing. It could be the first take.

How much prioritizing your life from day-to-day helps you become successful?

That is the most important thing because if you want to write songs, you must find time in your schedule. You have to make the time. Get up early, don't watch TV, don't watch movies, don't play video games. You need to make it a business. It's all a business. Even if you took one hour a day, you could get nothing done, or you could write two songs, but at least you've devoted that time to it.

Do you continue to learn all you can about your profession? If so, how?

The greatest university in the world is right there in your car or your iPhone or on Spotify. But for the aspiring musician, you have to be proactive in playing more than one style. Go to those radio stations, and they have every style picked out for you. You have to listen to what made it a hit. How many bars were in the intro? Where was the melody sung? Did they sing in the lower register or did they go up in the chorus? How many bars was the verse and the pre-chorus? You have to analyze it like a class in school. And if you treat it like that, you can have for free, the greatest teachers in the world. But you can't let your personal feelings get in the way, like saying "Havana" or "Macarena" was junk.

In any part of your life, has self-discipline played a major role in helping become successful? If so, how?

Yes.

Is there any factor, trait, or ingredient we may have omitted that helps in becoming a successful, hit songwriter?

Nothing we haven't already covered.

Do you believe a hit songwriter is born or made? Explain your thoughts.

Both. If you're born with it, it is easier. Some people like, Diane Warren work their asses off. Michéle Vice-Maslin is a machine, and Ken Hirsch was a machine. They just keep on doing it. They treat it like a business. Even if you don't write something great, you have to write something every day.

Do you believe talent is a gift or is it earned? Explain your thoughts.

I believe some people are gifted. You know that song, "God Must Have Spent A Little More Time on You." I believe some people are given a little bit of extra talent. But the people who have been the most successful have taken lessor talent and have worked their asses off to develop it. The person who works twice as hard is the one I want to be with because they treat every success like a major victory.

Do you believe that talent comes from within? If so, is it how they process stimuli in life?

For me, talent comes from thanking Jesus. There's no other answer to that. That's the gift from God.

Interview with Songwriter / Producer **Ted Perlman**

What is talent?

Talent is your ability to excel in one area or another.

Do you believe self-criticism helps or harms the success of a hit songwriter?

Every person in every creative field, whether you're a Steve Job at Apple, second-guessing yourself, "did we do the right thing in putting this out?" or Walt Disney with Mickey Mouse. Self-criticism is an important process in creativity to grow as long as you keep self-criticism in check. Otherwise, you'll never have any confidence in yourself.

Do you believe hit songwriters are more attuned to what is going on and happening around them than others?

I think hit songwriters are sometimes just lucky.

Do you believe inspiration is a state of mind, and could it be a major factor in the creation of a hit songwriter? Why?

Inspiration is the unexplainable like love. It's that which can't be proven. You could get fired, and that could inspire you to write the greatest love song in the world. You could be inspired by breaking up. Pain is a great inspiration. You have to be present and alert, although that dream state is a good way to receive inspiration.

Do you believe having empathy helps in becoming a hit songwriter? Explain.

Well, Allan Rich has had all his hits employing empathy of women. Gerry Goffin was the same way. For most men, if you asked them to write a song from a female perspective, they would write, "you suck, I hate you all."

LEFT TO RIGHT: Hit songwriter/producer, **Ted Perlman**, hit recording artist and actress, **Gloria Loring** and musician, **Rick Guetschow**.

Chapter Eleven:

Interview with Songwriter / Producer / Instrumentalist
Becky Buller

Hit singer-songwriter, producer and Instrumentalist, **Becky Buller**

Becky Buller is a multi-instrumentalist, singer, songwriter, and producer from St. James, Minnesota, who has traversed the globe performing bluegrass music to underwrite her insatiable songwriting habit. Her compositions can be heard on records by Ricky Skaggs, Rhonda Vincent, and Doyle Lawson & Quicksilver, to name just a few. Becky co-wrote "Freedom," the lead-off track of The Infamous Stringdusters 2018 Grammy-winning album Laws of Gravity. Two of Becky's co-writes are featured on 2019 Best Bluegrass Grammy-nominated albums: "The Shaker" (Travelin' McCourys) and "She Took The Tennessee River" (Special Consensus Rivers And Roads). Touring extensively with the Becky Buller Band, she recently released *"Crêpe Paper Heart,"* her 4th solo album, and her second recording on the Dark Shadow Recording label. It reached #1 on the August 2018 Bluegrass Unlimited Magazine Top 15 Bluegrass Albums chart. Becky is the recipient of 8 IBMA awards, including the 2016 Fiddler and Female Vocalist Of The Year and the 2018 Gospel Recorded Performance for the song "Speakin' To That Mountain." Equally passionate about bluegrass music education, Becky has 20 years' experience teaching fiddle, singing, and songwriting at workshops and camps around the world. She currently serves on the board of the IBMA Foundation.

Do you believe drive, passion, and stamina (energy level) play a major role in helping a person to become a successful hit songwriter? If so, how?

You must have an unquenchable fire in your belly to do this songwriting thing, or you'll definitely give it up at the first whiff of criticism or roadblock you face trying to get your songs heard.

Do you think work ethic plays a vital part in becoming a hit songwriter? If so, how?

It takes writing a ton of bad songs for every good one. You have to be dedicated. You have to want this as much as you want air and food.

How much does faith and belief in one's abilities help in becoming a hit songwriter? If so, how?

Often, you'll be the only one who believes you can do this and that's all you have to hang onto. But at least you have that! Keep believing! Keep writing! Keep recording! Keep pitching!

Interview with Songwriter / Producer / Instrumentalist
Becky Buller

How much of focus to detail and perfection helps make a hit songwriter? Why?

The best songwriters out there have a hyper-awareness of detail, what should be left in, what should be omitted. They're in tune with the song... pun intended. The song will tell you what it wants and needs, if you're listening.

What role does commitment to short and long-term goals affect success as a hit songwriter?

Each song is an investment. Each pitch is a gamble. The more you play, the more chances you have of winning. I've had cuts happen ten years after a song was pitched to an artist; the particular tune I'm thinking of became the title cut of that album!

Be deliberate about making lists of your goals, hanging them up where you can see them daily, marking them off as you reach them. Have a one-year plan; have a five-year plan. Often these lists are alive and fluid; update them as needed.

Here are some examples of short- and long-term goals for us songwriters:

I will write x amount of songs this year.

Who would I like to co-write with this year?

Who would I like to be co-writing within five years?

What do I need to do to make songwriting my primary source of income five years from now?

In five years, I would like to be up for the following awards:

What are some networking opportunities within my industry I can utilize to help me more efficiently meet my goals?

Do you believe that learning from failures and rejections help in becoming a hit songwriter? Please elaborate.

Of course! We always learn and grow the most during times of adversity. When it's going well, we tend to get too comfortable and take things for granted. Stay humble. Stay hungry.

Do you feel like being obsessive and persistent with writing help in becoming a successful, hit songwriter? If so, how?

It takes obsession and persistence to get good at anything. You've got to have intense drive and passion to make this happen.

Do you think taking risks in your career has helped you become successful? If so, how?

I'm not a huge risk taker. I tend toward being cautious. Looking back, I can see where I've missed opportunities because I'm that way. I can also see where I've avoided a lot of heartache.

I've always thought that achieving a lasting career in this industry would come from quietly plugging away at what I do, learning about what goes on in the background to make things happen, getting to know the folks who make it happen, etc.

That being said, there have been a few junctures (and I know there will be more) where I've had to hold my breath and jump. So far, it seems to have gone well, and I don't regret those decisions. If I had chosen another direction at those crossroads, would I be as happy? Quite possibly.

I trust God has a purpose for my life and is guiding me along the path to the places where He needs me to be when He needs me to be there. It's very rare that I get a clear answer on which way I need to go; it's not been an easy road. He doesn't promise me an easy road; He promises to be with me. And I know He is. It's been a good journey thus far.

Do you believe having a positive mental attitude, being optimistic, and possessing strong self-esteem play a major role in success? If so, how?

Optimism, positivity and good self-esteem are attractive things and are certainly assets to a successful writer and/or entertainer. In a world so increasingly overwhelmed by all things negative, those protecting positivity are really standing out. People are drawn to the light. Shine bright!

Does being a doer and not a talker help in becoming successful? If so, how?

Actions say more than words ever will. Show the powers that be what you can do. More than likely, they give you a chance to do more.

Does being a visionary or a dreamer help artists become successful? If so, how?

Sometimes...hopefully. You can have a vision for your art. You can bring that vision to fruition. But if you aren't surrounded by the right people at the right time, who will see it? What's the formula? How many parts faith? How many parts destiny? How much hard work? How much luck?

Do you think overall personality contributes to the success of a songwriter? If so, how?

A writer's personality will affect how they write, to a greater or lesser degree depending on how seasoned the writer is. We can't help but write ourselves into the songs we pen, even if sometimes we're the only ones who know we're in there. We view and write about the world through the lens of our experience. But the best writers are chameleons, assuming whatever personality necessary to best deliver the story they need to tell.

Do you feel patience and practice play a role in the creation of a hit songwriter? How?

To get good at anything, you must patiently practice it daily. Try not to practice the mistakes, of course.

How much prioritizing your life from day-to-day helps you become successful? If so, how?

I have lots of lists lying around...

Do you continue to learn all you can about your profession? If so, how?

If you're not continuing to learn and grow in your life in general and your profession specifically, then you're atrophying. And there are always ten or twenty folks behind you who are hungry, just waiting for you to lag so they can get ahead. I'm constantly picking up new tools and tricks of my trade, doing my best to mature and grow in my chosen profession. I do my best to share what I've learned; I'm very grateful to all the folks who have shared their experiences with me.

In any part of your life, has self-discipline played a major role in helping become successful? If so, how?

I'm a Christ Follower, which directly affects everything I do and all that I am. I try daily to live according to the Bible and maintain a self-disciplined personal life. God has blessed me greatly in so many ways, especially by giving me my husband, daughter and Tennessee family. I hope I'm a blessing to them and all the folks I come in contact with from day to day.

Interview with Songwriter / Producer / Instrumentalist
Becky Buller

Is there any factor, trait, or ingredient we may have omitted that helps in becoming a successful, hit songwriter?

Being a good listener. Listen to your industry. Listen to other genres of music. Listen to the music of your peers. Listen to folks' stories. Listen to yourself.

Do you believe a hit songwriter is born or made? Why?

I believe it to be an innate gift, something one has a preclusion to. It was always that way for me. It's the Jubal gene.

The coach and mentor in me say it can and must be cultivated to bear the best fruit.

Do you believe talent is a gift or is it earned? Explain your thoughts.

I think it can be gifted to those who want it bad enough that they're willing to pour their heart, soul, and very being into it. Honestly, if they want something that bad, they are probably born with a preclusion to it and a certain natural ability for it.

Do you believe that talent comes from within? If so, is it how they process stimuli in life?

I'm an extreme introvert. It's taken a lot for me to learn to be as outgoing in public as I am. Songwriting has always been my way of processing what's going on in my world. There's a degree of safety in being an observer, although it can be lonely.

What is talent?

Something woven into the very fabric of our souls that we have a natural tendency toward an affinity for. Something we were born to and for...Our purpose.

Do you believe self-criticism helps or harms the success of a hit songwriter? Explain.

Both. In the early stages of songsmithing, I think it's very important to turn off the self-editor and let things flow freely, generate content, ideas, and lines. Often, beginning writers are too quick to shoot an idea or line down as "dumb" when it may, in reality, be just what the song needs, albeit in embryonic form. Better to let it sit for a minute, hour, year, work on another portion of the song and come back around to the original thought.

After the song is almost complete, then it's important to go through every syllable and nuance. Did we say the same thing twice? Do those connector words really need to be in there? This is the time to be hypercritical.

Looking at the bigger picture, it's easy to be critical and get down on yourself when you see the success of your peers. Keep pulling yourself away from jealousy! Keep your eyes on the good things in front of and around you. Make a list of your successes and hang it next to your list of goals so you see it every day. Live in the center of and operate from this place of blessing.

Do you believe hit songwriters are more attuned to what is going on and happening around them than others? Please elaborate.

Everything in a songwriter's life...and that of those around the songwriter...is material. The best songwriter has his or her radar finely tuned to pick up on the next good idea, catchy phrase, gruesome story.

Do you believe inspiration is a state of mind and could it be a major factor in the creation of a hit songwriter? Why?

Learning to access the place within you where the music lives is critical. Being able to get there is definitely affected by all the chaos going on in your real world, whether you're hungry or thirsty, etc.

Interview with Songwriter / Producer / Instrumentalist
Becky Buller

Do what you can to prepare an environment where creativity is possible. Pick a physically and mentally comfortable place to write. Bring snacks; bring your beverage of choice. (I prefer to have coffee and chocolate handy.) Remember what works. Amend what didn't work this time the next time around. You'll get better at creating that space the more you work at it, whether preparing for a co-writing appointment or to simply write on your own.

Do you believe having empathy helps in becoming a hit songwriter? Explain.

We have to be able to relate with people to be allowed to sing into their lives. We are all ultimately writing for ourselves, to please, to bless, to exercise, to satiate... Even as we write for ourselves, we are writing for others. My details may vary slightly from yours, but The Human Condition is common to us all.

A professional songwriter must be able to write from whatever perspective is necessary to best convey the story or thought. It takes a healthy dose of empathy to step into those shoes.

ABOVE: **Becky Buller** and her Band.

RIGHT: **Becky Buller** receiving awards at the **IBMA.**

Chapter Twelve:

Interview with Songwriter / Artist **Jerry Vandiver**

Hit songwriter, **Jerry Vandiver**

Jerry's first major label cut, "Don't Waste It On The Blues," recorded by Gene Watson, reached #5 on the country charts in 1990, winning him an ASCAP award. In 1990, Wild Rose climbed the charts to #13 with Vandiver's penned hit, "Go Down Swingin'."

Since then, he had had two songs recorded by Tim McGraw, "It Doesn't Get Any Countrier Than This," featured on McGraw's platinum 6 CD "Not A Moment Too Soon," and "For a Little While," (reaching #2 on the country charts) on the quadruple platinum 1998 CMA Album of the Year, "Everywhere," winning Jerry a BMI Award. "For A Little While" was also included on McGraw's platinum 5 Greatest Hits CD and Special Edition Box Set.

Other artists recording Jerry's songs include Barbara Mandrell, Lee Greenwood, The Oak Ridge Boys, Phil Vassar, Dusty Drake, Lonestar, and David Lee Garza. Thanks to these artists, Jerry has songs on over 15 million records, and two of his titles are hanging on the wall in the Country Music Hall of Fame.

Jerry released his own CD in 2001 entitled "Don't Try This At Home." This critically acclaimed acoustic CD features a team of A-list Nashville players including the Grammy award-winning Fairfield Four (as seen in the movie, "O Brother, Where Art Thou?"

His highly-anticipated "Paddlesongs" CD, "True And Deep," "Songs For The Heart Of The Paddler" was released in the spring of 2011, followed by his newest release, an acoustic Americana CD, "I Wrote This One For You" in the fall of 2012.

Do you believe drive, passion, and stamina (energy level) play a major role in helping a person to become a successful hit songwriter? If so, how?

Absolutely. If you're not driven with a passion to express yourself in song, then you can't compete with those that have that drive and stamina.

Do you think work ethic plays a vital part in becoming a hit songwriter? If so, how?

Yes, very much so. Self-discipline in songwriting is tantamount to productivity, and this business likes those that are productive. I'm always amused by those who wait for the 4 am inspiration to write. I once heard a songwriter say "inspiration is for amateurs." I think there's a lot of truth to that.

Interview with Songwriter / Artist **Jerry Vandiver**

How much does faith and belief in one's abilities help in becoming a hit songwriter? If so, how?

If you don't believe in yourself, then who will?

How much of focus to detail and perfection helps make a hit songwriter? Why?

This is a tough one. I think when writing, the focus should first be on the message you want to convey and put that down. Then go over it again with attention to detail. One thing is for certain, if you're sloppy with the craft you are doing yourself and your audience a disservice and you are giving the powers that be a reason to say no.

What role does commitment to short and long-term goals affect success as a hit songwriter?

Good one. I've always believed in the long-term goal but firmly believe that the way to get there is the short-term goals in between. If you focus only on the long term (i.e., getting a #1 major label cut), you will trip over your own self not seeing the short-term goals before that – such as building your co-writer team, signing a single song contract, meeting people in position to help you, etc.

Do you believe that learning from failures and rejections help in becoming a hit songwriter? Please elaborate.

Learning from rejection. This business is not for the faint of heart. The secret is to take that rejection, try to figure out if there is, in fact, something truthful behind it and find that truth. That is, of course, after the sting of the rejection is less painful, and you can look on things with a more open mind. All that being said, there are two dangers: 1) having a closed mind/ego about being rejected. Attitudes like "screw these people, they're morons and have no idea what they are talking about" will do you no good. And 2) the exact opposite by taking that rejection as if it was the final word. I've had many, many songs recorded that were rejected by many powers that be. There's a fine line to walk between these two situations, and it comes with maturity and #3 above – believing in yourself.

Do you feel like being obsessive and persistent with writing help in becoming a successful, hit songwriter? If so, how?

There's also a fine line between obsessive and self-disciplined. I prefer self-disciplined. Write when you love it; write when you don't. But be good to yourself, too. There are many other important facets of life other than writing. A great writer is a complete human being.

Do you think taking risks in your career has helped you become successful? If so, how?

A songwriter by definition is a risk taker. I know lots of "songwriters" who aren't willing to jump in the deep end to make it happen. It doesn't happen in the shallow end of the pool.

Do you believe having a positive mental attitude, being optimistic, and possessing strong self-esteem play a major role in success? If so, how?

Yes, absolutely. It's easy to fall into a negative vibe in the midst of it all, but that will only keep you swirling in the black hole.

Does being a doer and not a talker help in becoming successful? If so, how?

The talkers outnumber the doers by a vast majority. I don't listen to talkers. They are a waste of time. What you do is your statement of your quality.

Interview with Songwriter / Artist **Jerry Vandiver**

Does being a visionary or a dreamer help artists become successful? If so, how?

Yes, but keep in mind not everyone – in fact, very few – will share or understand your vision or your dream.

Do you think overall personality contributes to the success of a songwriter? If so, how?

I've seen so many different types of personality in this business that I don't think that matters much unless it's an overwhelming negative one or egotistical, narcissistic one.

Do you feel patience and practice play a role in the creation of a hit songwriter? How?

Patience is not my virtue, and most songwriters are not patient with themselves, but there is also a fine line to be patient with yourself and the business and making things happen.

How much prioritizing your life from day-to-day helps you become successful? If so, how?

I'm not a good day-to-day prioritizing person, but I do believe organizing your day to write and work is important. Remember, this business loves productivity.

Do you continue to learn all you can about your profession? If so, how?

I'm always learning. I hear a melody or a great lyric or a new guitar riff and say, wow! I want to do that.

In any part of your life, has self-discipline played a major role in helping become successful? If so, how?

Self-discipline is the foundation of a successful songwriter. Yes.

Is there any factor, trait, or ingredient we may have omitted that helps in becoming a successful, hit songwriter?

The desire to make the song you write today better than the one you wrote yesterday.

Do you believe a hit songwriter is born or made? Why?

Both. I think some have an innate ability to observe the world and put it to lyric and music better than others. It still is hard work, however. But I feel that I personally am a prime example of "the harder I work, the luckier I get."

Do you believe talent is a gift or is it earned? Explain your thoughts.

Same as the answer to 18.

Do you believe that talent comes from within? If so, is it how they process stimuli in life?

Same as answer to 18.

What is talent?

I honestly don't know. I'm not a talented artist, piano player or ice skater. Maybe talent is the result of working inhumanely hard to perfect your passion for your craft?

Do you believe self-criticism helps or harms the success of a hit songwriter? Explain.

Self-criticism will help you beat the critics to the punch.

Do you believe hit songwriters are more attuned to what is going on and happening around them than others? Please elaborate.

Yes, I think so. Once your discipline becomes a natural

part of you, you will find yourself being much more observant to the world around you and the creative ideas that present themselves to you.

Do you believe inspiration is a state of mind and could it be a major factor in the creation of a hit songwriter? Why?

Inspiration is for amateurs.

Do you believe having empathy helps in becoming a hit songwriter? Explain.

I don't know if that it helps in becoming a hit songwriter, but it will help in becoming a better human being which might help you becoming a better songwriter.

Hit songwriter, **Jerry Vandiver** with his awards.

Chapter Thirteen:

Interview with Songwriter / Producer **Michéle Vice-Maslin**

Hit songwriter/producer, **Michéle Vice-Maslin**

Michéle Vice-Maslin is an Emmy Winning, #1 hit music producer/music arranger/ songwriter, music publisher who composes (both music & lyrics) and produces-arranges for artists/ films/television / ads/ promos/ games, etc. She has had numerous hit songs and cuts all over the world as well as over 5000 music placements. Her music can be heard on radio & television every day – 7-days-a-week/365 days-a-year.

Her first professional music production and next cut came shortly after when she produced SAM MOORE for the feature film "CAR 54: WHERE ARE YOU?" starring FRAN DRESCHER & ROSIE O'DONNELL. Not soon after that Michèle was taken under the wing of hitmaker producer NILE RODGERS (CHIC/ DAFT PUNK/ MADONNA/ROD STEWART, etc.) who mentored her, wrote with her and introduced her to some young writers he was working with.

Michéle wrote the #1 hit song "GET OVER YOURSELF" for EDEN'S CRUSH (WBS) also the theme song to hit TV series POPSTARS (WB), THE #1 hit song "CONTRIBUTION" for MICA PARIS (Feat. ERIC B and RAKIM) (Island), The International #1 hit single "HELP ME" from BACKSTREET BOY NICK CARTER (JIVE), the top 10 hit single "EVERY PART OF ME" from AMERICAN IDOL finalist LATOYA LONDON (PEAK/UNIVERSAL), the hit singles "FOREVER TONIGHT" and "ANOTHER WAY" from acclaimed Urban Jazz artist JONATHAN BUTLER. Songs for legendary soul artists SAM MOORE & JUNIOR WALKER. The theme song to the VIVICA FOX hit TV series MISSING performed by Atlantic Records urban artist KINA (Lifetime TV),

Songs for hit pop groups JUMP 5 (EMI/ CMG), NO SECRETS (Jive), PLUS ONE (Atlantic), AVALON (EMI/CMG), The hit Disney single "IF YOU ONLY KNEW", SAVANNAH OUTEN (Levosia/Radio Disney), Songs with Disney stars KAY PANABAKER, KENTON DUTY, ALLSTAR WEEKEND, Radio Disney artists CELICA WESTBROOK, Nickelodeon Star VICTORIA JUSTICE, to name but a few, as well as songs for film/TV incl. The hit film "SPLICE," QUEEN LATIFA'S" THE PERFECT HOLIDAY" UMA THURMAN'S "MOTHERHOOD," BAD GIRLS CLUB & many many others.

Michéle works out of her own studio Sweeter Songs East in Santa Monica, Ca. for her production company MOB FORCE and continues to enjoy her passion for producing, writing and publishing music.

She is married to hitmaker – acclaimed Producer /Engineer Harry Maslin (DAVID BOWIE, AIR SUPPLY/ MICHAEL JACKSON/ BAY CITY ROLLERS/ MELISSA MANCHESTER, ERIC CARMEN, JAMES TAYLOR, LOU REED, CARLY SIMON, BONNIE RAITT, HOT TUNA, etc.).

Interview with Songwriter / Producer **Michéle Vice-Maslin**

Do you believe drive, passion, and stamina (energy level) play a major role in helping a person to become a successful hit songwriter? If so, how?

I believe "drive, passion, stamina" play a major role in any endeavor one takes on including songwriting so I would say the answer is yes. Of course, one has to have "passion" as this business of music is so difficult that the only reason to pursue a creative career, as a creative such as a songwriter, is to do it for the love and passion of it and not any possible financial gain or fame, though that may come....and go.

"Drive" is also necessary as it is difficult at times to stay positive and keep moving forward amidst an endless sea of negativity and rejection that often surrounds a songwriter. Even "successful, "professional" songwriters.

As for "stamina" - Oh yes one must have endless boundless "stamina" as the life of a professional songwriter is very much 24/7 365 days a year. One must create and channel energy sources that don't even really exist as we must often create and finish that which we are creating on demand. One must have the stamina to rise above all the possible negativity as well.

Do you think work ethic plays a vital part in becoming a hit songwriter? If so, how?

If you mean "work ethic" as in running your world as a business, then yes, I do believe that it is very important for successful professional songwriters as in any other business.

How much does faith and belief in one's abilities help in becoming a hit songwriter? If so, how?

"Faith and belief" matter a whole lot. There are many, MANY, MANY "haters" and "bullies" trying to bring others down. Basically, that way they can think they will get ahead faster. So one must not listen to all that negativity and have faith and belief in themselves to keep the strength and the dream and keep moving always forward.

How much of focus to detail and perfection helps make a hit songwriter? Why?

"Focus and detail" are immensely important. I don't believe there is really any such thing as "perfection." We are all imperfect. I have a song called "Everyone's Imperfect." We can strive for perfection, nothing wrong with that and we may reach varying degrees of it here and there... and we may use the word "Perfect" to describe something, but it is only personal perfection. I don't believe perfection is real. We all have flaws and create flaws and that is what helps us grow and move forward. We are all sums of our "imperfections." Now "focus" that is imperative and "detail" too. One must be focused to keep on the path and not allow the negativity to derail the dream and the pursuit. One must pay attention to "detail" in songwriting to create fresh non-cliché lyric and melody details.

What role does commitment to short and long-term goals affect success as a hit songwriter?

For me, "Goals" are kind of like New Year's Resolutions...good to have, but I believe flexibility is key as goals are constantly changing and getting derailed. We can't be so hard on ourselves to accomplish all our goals. Sometimes we have to let go and go with the flow so to speak and see where the journey leads us. I wake up with plans for the day every day and end being sidetracked endlessly as the day progresses and this and that ends up taking priority over the initial goals I started out with.

As for long term goals they too are great to give and consider, but I think being open to what may come one's way and alter the goals is valuable too. If we are too focused on what we think our plans and goals are we might miss amazing opportunities.

Interview with Songwriter / Producer **Michéle Vice-Maslin**

Do you believe that learning from failures and rejections help in becoming a hit songwriter? Please elaborate.

"Rejection" – yes for sure. Songwriters and creatives experience rejection non-stop, so one best just brush it off and learn something if applicable from them and move forward as we have been discussing. "Failure" is basically relative, isn't it? It has varying degrees, doesn't it? Whatever "success" and "failure" is to each of us is different and changes all the time as we move through life. I do believe we learn the most from what we find to be our individual failures. Failure and success are very subjective and relative.

Do you feel like being obsessive and persistent with writing help in becoming a successful, hit songwriter? If so, how?

"Obsessive" no. I don't think that serves one well overall.

"Persistent" yes. But again, these terms are also subjective and relative and so different for each individual. "Persistence" goes back to tenacity and yes, a songwriter needs to have that for sure. It can be a very difficult windy road.

Do you think taking risks in your career has helped you become successful? If so, how?

I believe any time I have said "yes" and took a risk has helped for sure. Even if I didn't know how to really do the job at hand, saying "yes" to it has been the right and smart move. I have researched and pulled in experts and colleagues to accomplish the "yes" I took on. These were risky endeavors but a good thing. I have also said "no" on occasion and stayed in my comfort zone which I believe looking back was not perhaps always the best thing…but "it is what it is" as the saying goes and all of it is part of the journey so we mustn't look back. I like to keep moving forward and forgive myself, especially for those risks not taken. Forgiveness is also a big key factor.

Do you believe having a positive mental attitude, being optimistic, and possessing strong self-esteem play a major role in success? If so, how?

I believe that being positive is among the most important attributes to have overall in life actually! So yes! This business of Music is "Survival of The Fittest," and there is no other way to survive than to channel inner positivity and optimism. There is a lot of darkness swirling around, and so often we must be our own light to continue. As for "strong self-esteem" –yes… but not to the point of narcissism. LOL. Belief in one's self is always a thing for all endeavors. Unfortunately, in this biz, it is not uncommon to find that others do not believe in you and your abilities and talents so again one must look within and believe.

Does being a doer and not a talker help in becoming successful? If so, how?

Being a doer is a big yes! One is reliable if they are "doer" and get the job done.

Being a "talker" is a very different thing and can mean so many different things. I believe being communicative with co-workers and co-writes and "powers that be" is very important. Being talkative in terms of inspiring and empowering others, the same. Motivational speaking is a great thing. Now, if you mean a "talker" as in one who is just "all talk and no action" as the saying goes…then that is not the best attribute to have for sure. One must put their "words into action" and get going.

Does being a visionary or a dreamer help artists become successful? If so, how?

Well…having original ideas and dreams and aspirations for the future is always wonderful. I'm not sure it directly, necessarily, helps one become successful, but it is certainly a wonderful attribute to possess. It's a happy way to live for sure… and anything that is happy and positive is helpful. But again, success is relative and subjective depending on what success means to each individual person. In terms of "creatives" I know so many we would all consider uber "successful" who never feel that way and are always striving for more and more because they just never feel "successful" or "successful enough" and then vice-versa I know others who have had maybe what on paper does not seem like a lot of "success" yet they feel they are very "successful" and portray themselves as such. But back to being a dreamer and visionary…great stuff from which to create for sure.

Do you think overall personality contributes to the success of a songwriter? If so, how?

Hmmm - I'm not sure I understand this question. We all have different personalities in every aspect of life. I think we can only be true to ourselves and be who we are. Perhaps we need to work around our own personalities to not get in our own way. That would be optimum, but most people do get in their own way. That is human nature I believe. We all have our strengths and insecurities. I would say many creatives get in their own way. There are lots of insecurities and negativities at play. So then since we all are who we are, then I suppose our personalities come with us to our successes and failures. Did I answer the question LOL?

Do you feel patience and practice play a role in the creation of a hit songwriter? How?

I'm not sure what it means by "practice" …but "patience" for sure. It is very much a vocation of "hurry up and wait." Songwriters are always endlessly waiting… for the record to come out, for the movie to be released, for the tv show to air, for the feedback they need, for the info about the rewrites they may have to make, for their co-writers to get it together and stop canceling, for the artists to get it together and stop canceling, for the equipment in the studio to boot back up, for the production to finally be finished… and the biggest one… to get paid! … and so on and on and on.

By "practice" do you mean "practicing" one's instruments, one's vocals, ones writing and writing to get "better"? If so, then yes that is helpful and is usually developed naturally over years of crafting and hard work.

How much prioritizing your life from day-to-day helps you become successful? If so, how?

Well, this goes back to focus. But as the saying goes "If you want to make G-d laugh - tell him your plans." You can prioritize and plan all you want, but most days some things come along that rearrange one's priority list. Today for me it was a flat tire. Every day it is something. Being flexible and not too rigid to a schedule is a great thing. One must learn to go with the flow and not beat themselves up for veering off the path or plans. Sometimes by doing so amazing other things happen. That said though, if there are others involved such as for booked meetings, recording sessions, writing sessions, etc. One must prioritize those to be respectful and show up when scheduled and not inconvenience others.

Do you continue to learn all you can about your profession? If so, how?

Oh yes for sure. It's amazing how much this profession is changing every day. I subscribe to many, many industry newsletters and every day there is new technology, new laws, new music, new information, people changing positions, new companies being formed, others shutting down, new everything being shared. It's endless… I always want to learn new things about my profession. I believe it is very important to be up on the goings on. That is for me though. I know others who don't want to keep up and just want to create. Again, it goes back to… we can only be who we are.

In any part of your life, has self-discipline played a major role in helping become successful? If so, how?

Well, I do believe so. I am quite balanced and focused and disciplined and able to work under very stressful

Interview with Songwriter / Producer **Michéle Vice-Maslin**

conditions. I am able and often called upon to create on demand, so self-discipline plays a large part in that. Personally, for instance, you will most always find me in the daytime outside in the sun, on a lounge chair, in a bathing suit working. I have trained myself to be able to see the computer screen in the sun, and I am able to focus and not be distracted. I suppose that is one of my forms of self-discipline. During the evening I transition to inside to the studio. So yes, for me self-discipline plays a major role.

Is there any factor, trait, or ingredient we may have omitted that helps in becoming a successful, hit songwriter?

Yes! Thick Skin! This business of music and songwriting will wear one down. As I mentioned earlier in the interview, it is "Survival of The Fittest." Sometimes in an instant, I have seen people give up with one rejection. My motto is "Music Is My Air." It is what my learning seminars are called. I believe in order to survive as a professional songwriter it has to be one's "air." It is too difficult to navigate the system without that. It can be heartbreaking so one must breathe it to survive it. Remember "success" is relative. It means different things to different people, and in addition, it is constantly changing. In this business, as in many, one is only as good as their latest big thing ...or last "success." One can have a credit sheet a mile long and still has others deem that person not "successful" in their eyes. This is an area where one must again have thick-skin and believe in themselves and their successes. Is one successful because they make a lot of money? Is one successful because they have had a high charting song but make relatively little money from it? Is one successful because they have had one hit? Is one successful because they have tons of followers and fans? How many would deem them successful? Is one successful because they have sustained a career over decades even if they have not had a charting hit in years? Is one successful because they have had thousands of song placements? Is one successful because they are mentors and teachers nurturing new songwriters who then have gone on to have their "successes?" Is one successful because they make a living as a songwriter and every square of toilet tissue and everything else, they purchase is with funds made from their chosen vocation; here that being creating music. Is one successful because they can make their own schedule, only work with whom they want to, only take on projects they want to?... and on and on.... How do we measure success? Maybe it is simply that we can come home and have dinner with family for a while before going back to work. Maybe it is that we can take off on Sundays when we've always worked them before. Maybe it is when we are happy with our lives and our work and personally feel fulfilled and at peace. At any rate THICK SKIN is key!! Sorry to get off track.

Do you believe a hit songwriter is born or made? Why?

This is also a very subjective question. We are all born with talents towards many things. How we channel them and use them becomes our vocation. Often becoming a "hit" can be luck. Being in the right place at the right time. Getting the right opportunity. Writing and writing and persevering. Studying hit songs to see what the similarities and differences between them are. Listening and paying attention. There are endless variables that go into the endless possibilities.

Do you believe talent is a gift or is it earned? Explain your thoughts.

If one is spiritual, one would say talent is a gift. I believe...some divine grace. Talent appears in so many ways for so many things. I don't believe talent is "earned." I believe "success" in all its variations can be "earned" though sometimes it just lands on our plates without much effort or "earning." That is where luck comes in. I do believe some people are "luckier" than others for some reason and some have to work harder for what they want and receive.

Interview with Songwriter / Producer **Michéle Vice-Maslin**

Do you believe that talent comes from within? If so, is it how they process stimuli in life?

I believe talent comes from within and is then nurtured from within and without.

What is talent?

For this I had to look up the definition of "talent" in the dictionary as to me it is also subjective. The dictionary says:

"1a: a special often athletic, creative, or artistic aptitude
b: general intelligence or mental power: ABILITY
2: the natural endowments of a person
3: a person of talent or a group of persons of talent in a field or activity
4a: any of several ancient units of weight
b: a unit of value equal to the value of a talent of gold or silver
5 archaic: a characteristic feature, aptitude, or disposition of a person or animal."

"Talent" is found in many forms for many, many vocations in addition to songwriting. I'd like to think those of us who are professional songwriters have a "talent" for it –yes, but it is a "craft" so one can become better at it and develop their "talent" and skill by working at it and learning the craft as well.

Do you believe self-criticism helps or harms the success of a hit songwriter? Explain.

Well if "self-criticism" is looked at in a positive way as in "soul searching" then I do believe yes, it is good for all to know themselves and strive to know themselves better and constantly improve themselves so that they can improve the world around them as well. I don't think though that we should "beat ourselves up" for our errors and mistakes. We must try to stay positive and forgive ourselves and keep moving forward.

Do you believe hit songwriters are more attuned to what is going on and happening around them than others? Please elaborate.

I think that "Creatives" in general, not just songwriters are very attuned to their surroundings and goings on as they are constantly "on" - constantly creating. Everything is inspiration. So, I would say "yes" for songwriters for sure.

Do you believe inspiration is a state of mind and could it be a major factor in the creation of a hit songwriter? Why?

Yes, I do believe "inspiration" is a state of mind. As a successful professional songwriter, one must find inspiration in everything. One does not usually have the luxury of waiting on "inspiration" to arrive-one must have it. Professional songwriters are very often required to create on demand...channel artists, emotions, co-writers, assignments. One does not always have the luxury to have "writer's block." A professional songwriter must be able to create at a moment's notice and draw out inspiration from everything in them and around them.

Do you believe having empathy helps in becoming a hit songwriter? Explain.

I believe having empathy helps with everything, so yes, songwriting for sure. I believe songwriters need to have the ability to see the bigger picture, a rounder picture and be able to empathize with many personalities and situations. I believe "creatives" are usually greatly involved with deep thinking and soul searching and paying attention to the world without and within.

Chapter Fourteen:

Interview with Songwriter **Dee Moeller Moss**

Hit songwriter, **Dee Moeller Moss** with her husband, Wayne Moss.

Dee Moeller, the other half of the Moss household and Cinderella Studios, in its current form, has had an equally long and storied history in the music industry. Starting out at twelve years old, music has been a concentrated focus in Moeller's life for the majority of her seventy-eight years. With song credits under the billing of Willie Nelson, Waylon Jennings, Brenda Lee, and Wanda Jackson, Moeller has her own story to tell. Perhaps what is most remarkable about Dee Moeller, though, isn't her impeccable songwriting or the fact that she knows her way around a piano so well she can make it sing like an angel; it is the stillness in her spirit. Originally hailing from Roscoe, Texas, Moeller was a regular on the music scene before she had even started high school. "My family lived in Merkel, Texas, for a long time, but before we moved there, we lived in a little town called Roscoe, not too far from Snyder. Snyder had an amateur hour radio show on Saturday mornings. My parents took me down to audition when I was twelve, and KSNY kept me on as a regular so I didn't have to audition every week. I did that for about a year every Saturday morning before we moved to Merkel, and then it was a little too far to continue. When I was thirteen I had an audition set on the Big State Jamboree in Abilene, and it turned out pretty well, so they made me a regular on that. There were two bands who had shows in the area; Slim Willett, who wrote "Don't Let the Stars Get in Your Eyes" had one who did their show on Saturday mornings and another band, Fox Force Seven, who had their show on KRBC radio on Saturday nights. And then television came to Abilene, and I did that too, so I stayed pretty busy during my high school years."

During her time on television and radio in Abilene, Moeller found herself amid some of the greatest up and coming stars of the era. One such star was Elvis Presley, whom she opened for when he came to town because of her popularity and fan base in the community. "Since I was on television and radio so much in that area, I had a fan base there. Elvis was just getting started; he'd had a couple of good hits on Sun Records, and somebody booked him. I was fourteen at the time, and since I had a popular following, they booked me as his opening act. That was pretty exciting stuff for a fourteen-year-old girl. At the time I had never dreamed of becoming a songwriter, so I was doing copy material. There was a popular song at the time by Georgia Gibbs called "Tweedle Dee." I sang that song that night and later on Elvis, being new himself, didn't have a lot of his own stuff, so he was doing some copy material, too. Naturally, after I was through singing, I stood right off the stage behind the curtain so the audience couldn't see me, but I could see Elvis. He was so cute; he went out there and said: "Well, I'm going to do a song that's already been done." He looked over at me and winked and said: "Now she did it really well, but here's my version." So our audience heard "Tweedle Dee" twice that day."

She got to Nashville. Charles got her an appointment with Jim Denny to see if he'd start booking her on gigs." Moeller's lucky streak continued right on through her first meeting with Mr. Denny; when she arrived for her interview, she had an unexpected fan there in the form of MariJohn Wilkin, one of country music's finest songwriters. "MariJohn Wilkin was there when I went in to meet Jim Denny. She was from Winters, Texas, and her mother had told her about me because I made her think of Marijohn when she was young and playing around town back home. She recognized me and introduced herself, then took me into Jim's office for my appointment and told him about my background in Texas. After that, he started booking me, and I wound up on tours with Minnie Pearl, Stonewall Jackson, Don Gibson, George Jones, Skeeter Davis. A few different people."

With two such accomplished young artists in the same town, there was little chance that Moeller and Moss wouldn't run into one another sooner or later. When they were both still at the start of what would become long careers, Moeller and Moss met and dated for a time before going their separate ways. The two, alone, accomplished enough in their decades apart to deem both of them worthy of Legend's Corner. Their faces may not be in the mural just off of Broadway downtown, but the music they made has undoubtedly been weaved in and out of the fabric of Nashville for several generations.

Do you believe drive, passion, and stamina (energy level) play a major role in helping a person to become a successful hit songwriter? If so, how?

Yes. I think it takes all of those and I happen to have known Reba McIntire for a long, long time and the one thing she always says in interviews is something I totally agree with: "A lot of people have drive and stamina, but you have got to be willing to get up and work at it every day and do what you have to do to get it done. You can't give up. A lot of people do. It isn't easy. If it was easy, then everyone would be doing it, but you have to have all of those things and an absolute determination, and I think one more key ingredient is a strong enough belief in yourself that you can't be deterred by failure-if they can be called failures...or they can be called learning instances. It's not how many times you get knocked down its how many times you get up."

Do you think work ethic plays a vital part in becoming a hit songwriter? If so, how?

Yes, absolutely. You'll see interviews with songwriters, and they'll ask them about how many songs they have written, and they'll say 300 or so, but all 300 haven't been recorded unless you're The Beatles. I think the thing that makes the difference in making it happen is to be constantly learning and if you have some songs you think are good, but no one is recording them, I think it's a good idea to go back and take an objective look and see what the is song missing. The best songwriters never stop learning. I've had an occasion recently with Gretchen Peters doing a project here at Cinderella Studios, and I think she is one of the best songwriters. It's funny, when I find myself working on a new song, I've stopped and thought, "How would she approach this?" You can always learn from the best, whoever you think they are.

How much does faith and belief in one's abilities help in becoming a hit songwriter?

Faith and belief are everything.

How much of focus to detail and perfection helps make a hit songwriter? Why?

I tend to only write songs that are pretty much true

about somebody that I know, and when I get through writing the song, I tend to go back and see if the essence of that person is in there and if the poignancy or the sadness of the situation of them have been painted well enough. That's what I generally look for, but I have to say that I have been really, really blessed in that a couple of my very best songs, the ones I'm most proud of, just came to me in a moment. They just washed over me, and I was just the vehicle that wrote it down and went to the piano and found the melody. It was there for me. With those songs that take 30 minutes to write, sometimes don't even feel like you're doing it. I feel like those are a gift to me, and all my job was to write it down. That doesn't happen nearly often enough, but I'm grateful for the times it does.

What role does commitment to short and long-term goals affect success as a hit songwriter?

I didn't start out to be a songwriter. When I was three years old, I knew I wanted to be a singer that was all I focused on. When I came to Nashville, I came as a singer and had never written a song. I married and had a family and realized that it wasn't going to work out for me to continue as a singer to go on the road. I started trying to write. Fortunately, I was around people that were very encouraging to me, and I got a cut pretty quickly. I signed with Tree Publishing. I wrote a corny song called, "Beers and Tears," and every time went to do demos, Kris Kristofferson was at Columbia and different people that I met, kept encouraging me, telling me how good my songs were. That made a big difference to me in my learning to be a songwriter because I didn't come by it naturally. It was not something I intended to until I got to Nashville.

Do you believe that learning from failures and rejections help in becoming a hit songwriter? Please elaborate.

I've just been a very determined person. If I wanted something, I worked at it until I got it.

Do you feel like being obsessive and persistent with writing help in becoming a successful, hit songwriter? If so, how?

I am not a tunesmith. I can't really relate to people that make appointments every day to write. I did do that for a while with a couple of writers, and we wrote some really good songs, but I find I need something worthwhile to say, and it has to mean something to me, and I think that people who are not tunesmiths have a tendency to write that way. You know, if you're a guitarist or a pianist, you sit down and start playing a riff, it evolves into a feeling and thoughts I've been thinking about. I think everyone works differently at their craft, but to me, I've found that it works best if I'm just inspired but something real.

Do you think taking risks in your career has helped you become successful? If so, how?

I've always been a risk taker. I came to Nashville with unbelievable odds against me. In the 70's when my kids got a little older, I decided to put a band together and start doing live gigs, which I hadn't done in years and years. I think risks are necessary for growth and for accomplishments. I think if you get the status quo all the time, life gets pretty boring. It must be fun.

Do you believe having a positive mental attitude, being optimistic, and possessing strong self-esteem play a major role in success? If so, how?

Yes. When I first started writing and gained confidence, I got a lot of songs recorded, and then I went through a period where I kind of lost my confidence and I didn't get anything recorded. I've looked back on that period and thought that there were some things in my demeanor, at that time, that were not to my benefit. Confidence is very important.

Interview with Songwriter **Dee Moeller Moss**

Does being a doer and not a talker help in becoming successful? If so, how?

A lot of times people are just talkers. Their conversations are interspersed with a lot of excuses. Someone who is willing to walk the walk and do it; there are no excuses in their conversations.

Does being a visionary or a dreamer help artists become successful? If so, how?

I would have to say that Wayne is the visionary in the family.

Do you think overall personality contributes to the success of a songwriter? If so, how?

I think good social skills are imperative in life, whether you are an introvert or extrovert. If you have good social skills, you'll be okay.

Do you feel patience and practice play a role in the creation of a hit songwriter? How?

I think patience is really important.

How much prioritizing your life from day-to-day helps you become successful? If so, how?

In the past, I would get up, and everyone was out of the house, I would go to the piano. Now, I just wait for the mood to strike me. I'm not sorry for that. Just an observation, over the years, since knowing Wayne, I can see how brilliant he is. He works out everything in his head, and he sees it all; the notes the fingering—he sees everything and how it will work. Since he is such a brilliant musician, I'm sure that is the reason he has had so much success in songwriting.

Do you continue to learn all you can about your profession? If so, how?

Absolutely. There are a couple of new writers I'm drawn to, and I think they are phenomenal. I don't so much critique what they do but I buy their CD's, and I listen to their songs. I listen to how they went about telling their stories. How they go about saying it. I think everybody that is good and wants to be good is always trying to learn. I don't think you ever stop--if there is any quality to your craft at all.

In any part of your life, has self-discipline played a major role in helping become successful? If so, how?

Yes. When I decided to put a band together that took a lot of self-discipline. I was lucky to get a lot of young, hot players to play with me. I worked hard to keep up and be a leader.

Is there any factor, trait, or ingredient we may have omitted that helps in becoming a successful, hit songwriter?

Yes. Timing and luck. To me, that's the essence of the whole thing.

Do you believe a hit songwriter is born or made? Why?

I think everyone is born with gifts. Some people don't ever figure out what theirs are, but I think people in the arts have a tendency to be more aware of their gifts quicker. I think a hit songwriter can be made. I think you can learn a craft, but then you wonder if it wasn't there, to begin with, and you just figure out how to use it. I don't know—probably born.

Do you believe talent is a gift or is it earned? Explain your thoughts.

I think it's a gift. I don't think it necessarily has to be earned. I've known some unpleasant people that were very talented. They obviously had a gift.

Interview with Songwriter **Dee Moeller Moss**

Do you believe that talent comes from within? If so, is it how they process stimuli in life?

I think there is something in all of us that are stimulated by things. A thought, a deed, a sound, an emotion, an observance and that affects us inside. Our feelings and intuitions, our reactions...I guess I think we react to stimuli.

What is talent?

I sang before I spoke. I knew I was supposed to sing. I was four, ran down to a little café, sat down on a stool, and sang. I didn't ask anyone if I could, I just did it. I got a hamburger and a coke. That's when my mother was pregnant and was near her term. It was like—okay. I just knew when I was born. What that says about anything, I don't know. That's just the way it was.

Do you believe self-criticism helps or harms the success of a hit songwriter? Explain.

I think it's good if you do it in a productive way and don't get negative with it. There is a line there. There are many times when I should have re-written, and I didn't. You have to critique yourself.

Do you believe hit songwriters are more attuned to what is going on and happening around them than others? Please elaborate.

Absolutely. I think that some of the songs that I'm drawn to are the ones that are so aware of the surroundings that the lyrics paint a picture. You almost feel like you're in the space with them. I'm an avid book reader. I like the authors that write their prose so intimately that as you're reading, that you feel like you are sitting in that room, in a chair, across from that person. I think really, really good songwriters are more attuned to their surroundings.

Do you believe inspiration is a state of mind and could it be a major factor in the creation of a hit songwriter? Why?

I think it could be a state of mind. If you are really aware of what is going on around you and in the world, I think there are little surprises that come up that you would never have thought of if you hadn't been paying attention to something that comes by you in some form—television, movies, newspapers, books... I'm a people watcher. It's amazing the thoughts you can get. I think by being aware, there are inspirations that will come to you that are unexpected. They are there for the taking if you are available.

Do you believe having empathy helps in becoming a hit songwriter? Explain.

I feel very strongly about empathy. I'm never one to brag on myself, but if I have one quality to talk about, is that I have deep empathy for the world. There are things that I see that I've never experienced in my life, but somehow, I understand it and can relate to that issue. It does affect what I write. I wish it was something everyone had in them. I think it would be a great tool in the world.

Chapter Fifteen:

Interview with Producer / Songwriter / Musician **Wayne Moss**

Wayne Moss pictured with his wife, Dee Moeller Moss

A West Virginia, soft-spoken steady-handed man: Wayne Moss was born in 1938 and would waste little time on his journey to making music his life. "My mother's originally from Cottontown, Tennessee and my dad is from Russellville, Kentucky. They met here in Tennessee and worked at DuPont together in 1925. Moss ended up coming here [Nashville] in 1959 to stay. It was in 1953, however, that Moss would give his first audition in town, and receive his first no–an answer that quickly grew rare in his career. "I came down here when I was fifteen and did an audition with Chet Atkins. My mother was there, and she said to Chet 'Isn't he amazing?' Chet said 'No, he's average, but maybe he can get a job at the Opry or something.' My mother told him music was all I knew and asked what he'd have me do. Chet responded with 'I don't know, he looks like he'd make a good plumber.' Chet didn't figure it was up to him to figure out my career. For many people, that would crush their spirit, but all it did was piss me off. I made a concerted effort to make Chet Atkins hire me for a whole lot of sessions after that, and he did. He even cut four of my songs and came out to record at Cinderella."

To hear Moss tell the story of how he came to music as a career, one would think he was making a simple decision like what to eat for dinner, or which shoes to wear out dancing. Moss maintains that casual tone and calm demeanor in everything he does, whether he is sipping coffee, explaining how his Flickinger console works, or quietly harmonizing with his wife, Dee, at the kitchen table. To Moss, it was a simple decision. When nothing else seemed palatable, Moss found music. "My dad worked in a chemical plant in West Virginia, and I didn't want to do that; there were coal mines in the area, and I didn't want to do that either. My dad had me help him deliver coal, and that also wasn't any fun, so my mother encouraged me to pursue music. I started out with piano lessons when I was very young, and I didn't care for that. My daddy bought me a six-dollar guitar when I was eight, and I've been playing it ever since."

Before Cinderella Studios was established as a recording studio, Wayne Moss spent time working as a session musician for hire with several labels including Phillips, RCA, Columbia, and Bradley's Barn in Mount Juliet, just outside of Nashville. Some of his most notable years as a session musician were spent alongside Dolly Parton and Porter Wagoner at RCA, though they certainly weren't the only artists he worked with. Moss' record includes Roy Orbison, Tammy Wynette, and Bob Dylan. When asked what it was like as a young man playing behind Parton and Wagoner, Moss let out a quiet laugh. "It was a lot of fun. Dolly and Porter were both practical jokers; Felton Jarvis had an anaconda that he turned loose in the studio one day. There was a whole strings section, and I was sitting there playing guitar with them. They were all sitting there raising their feet up off the ground. I finally saw what it was—about a twelve-foot-long snake. We had a lot of fun together." In addition to Parton and Wagoner, Moss spent two years playing alongside country music maven, Brenda Lee, and Charlie McCoy & The Escorts, doing live gigs and recording demos throughout the late 1950's and early 1960's.

The reality of a session musician's life can be as tiring as it is exciting, and after twelve years on Music Row, Moss was ready to slow things down. "I spent twelve years playing with Dolly and Porter and everybody else. That'll wear you out: four sessions a day, five or six days a week. I got to the point that I couldn't do it anymore. A lot of times my day would start at 10:00 AM and end after a 10:00 PM session was over. There's no way to stay alert with that kind of schedule. We drank a lot of coffee, smoked a lot of cigarettes, and most the time we'd knock out anywhere from four to six songs in a session. That's tiring. Bob Dylan came to town, and we cut one song a week. He wasn't in any hurry at all, and that was a nice change of pace for a little while." Cinderella Studios came to life not long after that, but not without protest from Moss' colleagues.

"One day after I quit I got a call. It was Porter and Dolly and Felton Jarvis on separate phones saying "what do you mean you quit doing sessions?" I told them I wanted to do my studio and pursue my own band, Barefoot Jerry. Another day I got a call from Felton, and he said: "hey man you've got to come down and do Elvis." I told him, no, and he said, "But it's Elvis." I said, "I don't care, I don't want Porter and Dolly to think they're less important." Next thing you know, I had Chet Atkins out here recording in my studio with Mickey Newbury. We cut a lot of good records out here. We cut the original of "Delta Dawn", we cut the first record of "American Trilogy" by Mickey Newbury, we cut the first record of "Burnin' Love." We've done a lot to help Elvis' career without ever doing that session."

Though Moss got his start in country music, his recording studio is not limited to one genre. What started as a good reputation by word of mouth eventually brought bands and musicians from far and wide to the front doors of Cinderella Studios. "KISS came because I recorded Steve Miller Band and they liked the way it sounded. Steve Miller and Linda Ronstadt were on Capitol Records at the time, and they recommended us—they knew me, and they told other people they needed to record here. Steve Miller is a good example of that; he was trying to cut on the West Coast, and there was so much partying going on he couldn't get anything done. He had his first song here done in forty-five minutes, and he knew this was where he needed to be. He told Linda this was the place to go, and Linda ended up cutting Silk Purse, the whole album, and "Long Long Time," as a single, out here."

Alongside the launch of Cinderella Studios, Moss pursued his own music, first with a band of session musicians under the name Area Code 615, then Barefoot Jerry. "Area Code 615 came about while we were cutting The Monkees at RCA. Mike Nesbit told us he needed to work on some lyrics and to take five. On that break, I said somebody should play something. David Briggs started playing "Lady Madonna" on the piano. There was a banjo, a fiddle, and a steel guitar and we all started playing along with Briggs. I said we need to cut an album like this and everybody chimed in." Area Code 615 began with an album at Polydor Records with the unique sound of 70's hits performed by traditionally country sounding instruments. "Polydor, our label, sent a guy from William Morris up in New York down to see us and ask how many dates per year we'd like to work. We all said none because we were making a killing in sessions at the time. He advised Polydor to drop us, and right after they did, we were nominated for a Grammy for Best Instrumental Group of the Year in 1970. We were up against Ferrante & Teicher, Henry Mancini, Boots Randolph, and Blood Sweat and Tears. Blood, Sweat, and Tears won that year, but Henry Mancini lost too, so it's alright." After they were dropped from Polydor, Charlie McCoy, Kenneth Buttrey, Mac Gayden, and Wayne Moss would go on to form Barefoot Jerry. Together with a total of forty-five members rotating in and out, the band produced ten albums, charted, and saw critical acclaim for their work.

Do you believe drive, passion, and stamina (energy level) play a major role in helping a person to become a successful hit songwriter? If so, how?

Yes. The only difference between a hit songwriter and one that doesn't succeed is they give up. First song I ever wrote, which was a horrible song, got cut by The Hilltoppers.

Do you think work ethic plays a vital part in becoming a hit songwriter? If so, how?

The work ethic is about how many times you get up. I had an interview with Chet Atkins when I was 15, and he told my mother, "No, he's not wonderful. He's average." That could either crush your spirit or make you mad. It made me mad enough to stay at it till I ended doing most of the RCA sessions that Chet hired me for. So, it can either be learning experience or a deterrent, depending on how you go about it. Songwriting is the same way, Harlan Howard said for every song he gets cut, he gets 99 turned down. Mickey Newberry once said, when he feels good, he plays golf, when he feels bad, he writes a hit.

How much does faith and belief in one's abilities help in becoming a hit songwriter?

Well, I dealt with a lot of faith in my book. Been going to the same church for 30 years. The Lord brought Dee and I together at just the right time, and now we are co-writing. Faith and belief are absolutely everything.

How much of focus to detail and perfection helps make a hit songwriter? Why?

My favorite song I've ever written is called, "If There Were Only Time for Love." Took me one year to write that and it was a chart record by a lot of people. The only Barefoot Jerry song that ever got in the charts was "You Can't Get Off with Your Shoes On," and that took 30 minutes to write, so it depends on the lyrical content. When you know what you want to say, it just comes.

What role does commitment to short and long-term goals affect success as a hit songwriter?

Well, my mother once said, "what do you want to do when you grow up?" and I said, "I don't know, I'm a kid, leave me alone." She kept on until I finally said, "Okay, I want to go to Nashville and be like Chet Atkins and have a studio. I've done those. Took a few years. I got here in 1959, but I made that commitment when I was 15. That commitment truly affected my success.

Do you believe that learning from failures and rejections help in becoming a hit songwriter? Please elaborate.

My mother built my self-esteem from first day I picked up an instrument. I'd be tuning my guitar, and she'd say, "That's so pretty." She convinced me I could do things that I wasn't even capable of and so it was impossible for anyone to convince me otherwise or that I was worthless.

Interview with Producer / Songwriter / Musician **Wayne Moss**

Do you feel like being obsessive and persistent with writing help in becoming a successful, hit songwriter? If so, how?

I'm not one of those people that can sit down and make myself write. I have to have inspiration fall out of the sky and say, "that would make a good song." As opposed to sitting down and trying to turn out product every day. I've only co-written with two or three people, and I know there are folks that do that every day for a living. Some people are very successful at that. I pitched a song to Chet Atkins, and he sat on it for five years before he cut it. It takes a long time. A good song will rear its head eventually. You can't keep a good song down.

Do you think taking risks in your career has helped you become successful? If so, how?

At the peak of my recording career with the Nashville A-Team as a session player, I decided to pull the plug and peruse my Area Code 615 and Barefoot Jerry Band and run my studio Cinderella which was taking a big risk. I was making good money playing on everyone else's records. There was a lot of stress involved, smoked a lot of cigarettes, which didn't do a lot for my health, but I'm a lot happier running a studio, songwriting, and pursuing the Barefoot Band.

Do you believe having a positive mental attitude, being optimistic, and possessing strong self-esteem play a major role in success? If so, how?

Yes. You can say you need to have a certain amount of humility, but I think people are going to relate to you better if you have enough ego to look like you're enjoying what you're doing when you perform and if you write positive songs and so on. I think there is a certain amount of ego that you need. I've heard people say that there are folks that need two airplane tickets, one for themselves and one for their ego. You need a good amount of self-esteem that nobody can break down.

Does being a doer and not a talker help in becoming successful? If so, how?

I know a lot of people who are always "fixing to do" a lot of things but never get around to doing anything. You're better off having small goals and following through with them before you go to the next one.

Does being a visionary or a dreamer help artists become successful? If so, how?

I don't know if it helps you with your success or not but I try to look ahead to things. I've written two or three songs that I'm very passionate about. I've written about things in the 1970's that either have happened or about to happen; I'm very adamant about certain things in my writing. I do tend to be a visionary.

Do you think overall personality contributes to the success of a songwriter? If so, how?

I don't know. I guess you must be personal enough to have the confidence to go up to a publisher or artist that the song is the greatest thing since sliced bread-whether it is or not. If you are friendly and don't act like you know everything in the world. If you feel like you have the best interest of the artist at heart and not thinking about how much money you could make. Thanking people goes a long way—it pays to be friendly.

Do you feel patience and practice play a role in the creation of a hit songwriter? How?

Depends on the song you're writing. Some songs could take a year trying to get every single word right, and then there are songs that fall out of the sky in 30 minutes-which don't take a lot of patience. If you are trying to say something that's never been said before, it's going to take a little longer.

Interview with Producer / Songwriter / Musician **Wayne Moss**

How much prioritizing your life from day-to-day helps you become successful?

In the twelve years of session playing that I did, I would not rehearse very much. I'd think of licks in my head but rather than play them over and over; I'd wait till I got to the session. That way it was new and fresh. "Only Daddy That'll Walk the Line" is a good example.

Do you continue to learn all you can about your profession? If so, how?

Yes. I try to learn from good songwriters. I grew up idolizing B.B King and people like him, but I missed a few along the line. I continued to be inspired by good songwriters and players. Not enough that I steal from them, but they inspire me enough to broaden my horizons.

In any part of your life, has self-discipline played a major role in helping become successful? If so, how?

I had a lot of self-disciple in the 12 years I had on the row. A lot of times I'd be doing four sessions a day-five, sometimes six days a week. That takes a lot of coffee and determination. It's really hard to come up with licks that are new and fresh, yet old and familiar at the same time. Quite a bit of strain involved with the many different types of sessions I was involved in. I got a lot gray hair with the Barefoot Jerry Band. We went through 40 musicians in the 10-11 years working the road. When we lost a musician, we would have to start all over and teach them the songs, and I sure learned the songs myself. It was time-consuming and had to be disciplined to not throw in the towel.

Is there any factor, trait, or ingredient we may have omitted that helps in becoming a successful, hit songwriter?

Knowing the right people.

Do you believe a hit songwriter is born or made? Why?

I think they are born. The really good ones…like Kris Kristofferson, Harlan Howard, Mickey Newberry, etc. They thought about the punchline before anyone else.

Do you believe talent is a gift or is it earned? Explain your thoughts.

I used to have a plaque that said, "Your life is a gift from God. What you do with it is a gift to God." It's a good reason to write positive songs. I think it's a gift.

Do you believe that talent comes from within? If so, is it how they process stimuli in life?

I think talent is God-given. You can use it or throw it away.

What is talent?

To me, it was digging deep within myself. Once I said the words out loud of what I wanted to do, I had to do it. Goals. Talent comes with goals. I couldn't change my mind because I said what I wanted to do. It didn't happen till my mother made me say what I wanted to do.

Do you believe self-criticism helps or harms the success of a hit songwriter? Explain.

I've heard a lot of people say; I'm my own worst critic. I think it's a device to shoot for higher goals-being a perfectionist.

Do you believe hit songwriters are more attuned to what is going on and happening around them than others? Please elaborate.

Yes. There's been a lot of songs that were written during the wars, people getting killed, current events; etc.

Interview with Producer / Songwriter / Musician **Wayne Moss**

Do you believe inspiration is a state of mind and could it be a major factor in the creation of a hit songwriter? Why?

I guess there are varying views on that. I've heard that success is 1% inspiration and 99% perspiration. I tend to write from inspiration as opposed to picking out something from thin air and writing about it. I don't do as well that way.

Do you believe having empathy helps in becoming a hit songwriter? Explain.

Yes, if you see something wrong in society, you can write about how to make it better. There are things that occur--you can be kind about it—don't be forceful and crush someone's spirit. There's only time for love in this world.

Chapter Sixteen:

Interview with Songwriter **Tom Snow**

Hit songwriter, **Tom Snow**

Tom Snow has been making music, recording albums, and writing hits - on record, on the radio, in the United States and all over the world - for over thirty years.

He has twice been nominated for the Academy Award for Best Song from a Motion Picture: "Let's Hear It For The Boy" from Footloose (1984) and "After All" from Chances Are (1990); and he has been nominated twice for the Grammy Award: Song of the Year - "Don't Know Much", Best Album of Original score written for a Motion Picture - Footloose soundtrack. He was also nominated for the Tony Award in 2000 for the Broadway show Footloose. He won the Emmy in 1998 for Outstanding Main Title Theme Music - Fame-L.A.

He has released four solo albums: "Country" (Atlantic Records, 1971), "Taking it All in Stride" (Capitol Records, 1975) "Tom Snow" (Capitol Records, 1976) and "Hungry Nights" (Arista Records, 1982).

Tom's scoring work has appeared in films (Chances Are), and on television (Pee Wee's Playhouse, Steel Magnolias, Teech, Grand, etc.) He has added songs to numerous motion pictures including Footloose; Lion King II; Honey, I Shrunk the Kids; The Butcher's Wife; All the Right Moves; Two of A Kind; Heart Like A Wheel; Oliver and Company; and Sing, among others.

The biggest stars in the world have recorded Tom's songs, including Barbra Streisand, Christina Aguilera, Tina Turner, Cher, Diana Ross, Bonnie Raitt, Linda Ronstadt, Ray Charles, Kenny Loggins, Gladys Knight, Bette Midler, George Benson, and Selena. Tom Snow's hit songs have been repeatedly honored with BMI Citations of Achievement for their radio popularity. Songs like, "Love Sneaking Up On You" (Bonnie Raitt), "Don't Know Much" (Linda Ronstadt and Aaron Neville), "He's So Shy" (Pointer Sisters), "Dreaming Of You" (Selena), "If Ever You're In My Arms Again" (Peabo Bryson), "Somewhere Down The Road" (Barry Manilow), "You Should Hear How She Talks About You" (Melissa Manchester), "Good For Me" (Amy Grant), and "Make A Move On Me" (Olivia Newton-John)

In 1986, Tom won the prestigious Robert J. Burton Award for BMI's Most Performed Country Song of the Year - Dolly Parton's "Don't Call It Love."

Tom's recent projects embrace the world of pop music (DJ Meck's #1 European remix smash "Thunder In My Heard. Again"- 2005), a song on Joe Cocker's 2002 release ("Love Not War"), songs on both Christina Aguilera's English and Spanish language albums (with sales of 9 million and 3 million, respectively), songs on Barbra Streisand's and Johnny Mathis's last two Christmas albums, and a 2008 re-recording of He's So Shy" by The Stunners for the hit TV show iCarly.

Interview with Songwriter **Tom Snow**

Tom graduated from the Berklee College of Music with a degree in Composition. He received their Distinguished Alumnus Award in 2000. He is a member of the Academy of Motion Arts and Sciences.

Do you believe drive, passion, and stamina (energy level) play a major role in helping a person to become a successful hit songwriter?

Absolutely. These three traits are key to making your way into the world of hit songwriting. You need all three at the beginning, middle and final stages of your career. Lose one of them, and you should retire or seek a different career. Put together; these qualities define a true professional in any field of endeavor.

Do you think work ethic plays a vital part in becoming a hit songwriter? If so, how?

Work ethic is another way of describing discipline. As the saying goes: "Half of life is showing up." It takes a strong work ethic and real discipline to do that day-in, day-out over the span of a career.

How much does faith and belief in one's abilities help in becoming a hit songwriter?

I'm not sure that these are necessarily inherent. I know in my case they weren't. I had to use the four previous qualities to build that kind of confidence. I also believe insecurity can be an artist's motivation to succeed because it sucks to be insecure.

How much of focus to detail and perfection helps make a hit songwriter?

Focus to detail is a must. That's why I did so much rewriting. In the heat of creating, you can't let yourself be hobbled by perfection. Few compositions come out fully formed, and most require some "post-birth" tweaking. Some of the best art is accidental and trying to perfect it is essentially impossible. Write and rewrite!

What role does commitment to short and long-term goals affect success as a hit songwriter?

The best short-term goal I know of is a deadline. You just gotta get it done. Long-term goal...make enough money to retire well.

Do you believe that learning from failures and rejections help in becoming a hit songwriter? Please elaborate.

No question about it. Failure is the greatest teacher. It takes a while to learn how to deal with it and make it work for you, but you will benefit immensely from acquiring the ability., The last thing professionals need to hear is constant praise. Writing for the marketplace is very different from writing for yourself. On the other hand, encouragement given at the right time goes a long way.

Do you feel like being obsessive and persistent with writing help in becoming a successful hit songwriter? If so, how?

Just as a professional athlete trains obsessively and persistently to hone their skills, so must a commercial songwriter. In my case it was unavoidable. The more I learned, the more I knew I needed to learn. It's a sense of divine discontent that fuels the process. And the process never stops.

Do you think taking risks in your career has helped you become successful? If so, how?

Just pursuing a career in music is a big risk. Fortunately, being 21 and dumb enough to try was a blessing for me. Looking back, I can't imagine how I did it. Sink or swim, I guess.

Do you believe having a positive mental attitude, being optimistic, and possessing strong self-esteem play a major role in success? If so, how?

If you're lucky enough to be born with all three in DNA then, yes, I believe they help enormously. If you're not lucky to possess such character traits… a good psychiatrist can help fill the void.

Does being a doer and not a talker help in becoming successful? If so, how?

All talk and no walk rarely work, but one still has to do some amount of self-promotion. I always found the latter to be tedious, but I was fortunate in having collaborators who excelled in the field.

Does being a visionary or a dreamer help artists become successful? If so, how?

I can't really say. I don't think of myself in those terms unless I'm under the influence of some outside agent in which case I'm of no use to anyone.

Do you think overall personality contributes to the success of a songwriter? If so, how?

I believe personality has little to do with the creative process. Much of the most beautiful and important music has been created by grumpy people. Writing can do that to you. It's difficult and self-centered. On the other hand, having a pleasant personality makes collaboration a lot easier, and collaboration generally produces a better product.

Do you feel patience and practice play a role in the creation of a hit songwriter?

Absolutely. Practice improves your craft and patience allows you to practice.

How much prioritizing your life from day-to-day helps you become successful?

All I did was write for 35 years. I guess that's prioritizing. In any case I never consciously prioritized.

Do you continue to learn all you can about your profession? If so, how?

I am retired from writing so I can't really answer that question with any relevance. I did a lot of "studying" by listening to songs I wish I'd written. My musical education at Berklee College of Music (class of '69) gave me the tools to analyze all facets of songwriting/composing: harmonics, phrasing, space, prosody, etc. Apart from that, my years in the Biz taught me all I wish to know.

In any part of your life, has self-discipline played a major role in helping become successful? If so, how?

Yes, Self-discipline is essentially the same thing as a strong work ethic.

Is there any factor, trait, or ingredient we may have omitted that helps in becoming a successful, hit songwriter?

I think you've covered the most important points.

Do you believe a hit songwriter is born or made? Explain your thoughts.

Songwriting is a craft that must be learned and constantly practiced. I don't think birth has much to do with it. That said, children of musical parents are more likely to be innately musical.

Do you believe talent is a gift or is it earned? Explain your thoughts.

Talent is a gift, but it can also be "earned." You come

Interview with Songwriter **Tom Snow**

into this world with natural gifts, and it's up to you to decide whether to exploit and strengthen them.

Do you believe that talent comes from within? If so, is it how they process stimuli in life?

(A) Yes. (B) Perception of outside stimuli depends on many factors: gender, race, ethnicity, culture, etc. These factors compel the individual to process outside information in a personal way which then influences whatever expression one puts forth, be it music, painting, writing, etc.

What is talent?

A natural proclivity enhanced by thousands of hours of practice. (A great read on this is "The Talent Code" by Daniel Coyle. Recommend it!)

Do you believe self-criticism helps or harms the success of a hit songwriter?

It's a double-edged sword. Being honest with yourself when assessing your work is a good thing. Too much nit-picking is harmful.

Do you believe hit songwriters are more attuned to what is going on and happening around them than others?

Most songwriters spend their waking hours in a room alone or with a collaborator. I doubt they are more attuned than others to the outside world.

Do you believe inspiration is a state of mind, and could it be a major factor in the creation of a hit songwriter? Why?

Definitely. I developed a habit of getting on my knees before starting a day's writing and asking for an "open channel." More than anything, inspiration is a product of hard work, patience, and faith. And then, you gotta be ready when it strikes!

Do you believe having empathy helps in becoming a hit songwriter? Explain.

I never really thought about this is a way that's specific to songwriting. I believe having empathy makes you a better person. I can't see how it's terribly relevant to the creative process. As I've said before, it's a very self-involved process.

Chapter Seventeen:

Interview with Songwriter **Wil Nance**

Hit songwriter, **Wil Nance**

Wil Nance hit the top of R&R and *Billboard* with his #1 Brad Paisley smash, "She's Everything," a song on Time Well Wasted, the multi-platinum, 2007 CMA Album of the Year.

In 1999, Wil received a BMI award for "Round About Way," a #1 hit single for George Strait, a song on the multi-platinum, CMA Album of the Year, Carrying Your Love With Me. "Round About Way" is also on George Strait's, Latest Greatest Hits and Strait's, 50 Number Ones...Over ten million sales and counting.

He also landed on Tourbadour, George Strait's platinum-selling, Grammy-winning, 2008 CMA Album of the year with a song called, "If Heartaches Were Horses," (Nancy, Brock/Dillon.)

In 2009, George Strait cut another song by Nance, "Where Have I Been All My Life?" (Nance/Williams/Austin), which is on the CD, Twang. In 2015, "It Takes All Kinds" (Nance/Regan/Strait/Strait) on the CD, Cold Beer Conversations.

Nance is currently signed with Curb Publishing and has two new cuts on Curb Record's artist, Mo Pitney and a new cut on Tim McGraw.

Do you believe drive, passion, and stamina (energy level) play a major role in helping a person to become a successful hit songwriter? If so, how?

Yes, very much so. In my case, it takes a lot of energy to write songs. You definitely have to be passionate about it. You got to love what you're doing and try to do it the best you can. Perseverance, you must have to stamina and perseverance in this business. I've seen a lot of talented people leave this town (Nashville) because they didn't persevere long enough. Some of the less talent folks became successful because they persevered. They had the stamina to hand around and see what could happen. You have to be thick-skinned as well. Believe in what you do.

Do you think work ethic plays a vital part in becoming a hit songwriter? If so, how?

Definitely. I think that's what they call a brief-case writer, where you get up every day, and you go downtown to a room or at your house, and you become very disciplined in the creative sense. You get up every day, and you go into work, and you try to create. I think if someone is paying you to be a songwriter, you can't wait around for inspiration to strike—whether you are getting paid or not; you can't wait for it to write songs. Back in the day, the guys like Merle Haggard, they wrote when they were inspired, but I think if you are going to be a staff songwriter, you have to have good work ethic and be very disciplined.

Interview with Songwriter **Wil Nance**

How much does faith and belief in one's abilities help in becoming a hit songwriter?

I think you always have to believe that God made you... It's funny, I remember when I first moved to town, and I saw a man named Gary Burr at The Bluebird, and he blew me away. I walked out of there impressed and depressed at the same time. I thought, what am I doing here? That's where the faith in yourself comes into play. You gotta believe that God made one Wil Nance and one YOU. You have to believe in what you do and create something only you can create. So, I walked out of The Bluebird after hearing Gary Burr sing all those hits and the next morning, I woke up and went, one day I'm going to write a song he (Gary Burr) wishes he'd written. I think that's where the faith yourself comes in--whether you are writing country songs or spiritual songs. You must believe you are here for a purpose. Self-esteem and integrity. This town will rob you of those things if you let it.

How much of focus to detail and perfection helps make a hit songwriter? Why?

I've always been a bit of perfectionist especially when it comes to the lyric. I've always been pretty picky about my lyrics and wanted to write songs "to the wall," write them where they are really written well. There are two theories to that--the other theory is: write them in a hurry and see what happens. I've done that before, too. You know I think, more than anything you have to have fun. You know, I'll say this, I've never had success with anything, looking back on it, that I didn't have fun with it. It's weird how that happens. I think another songwriter pointed that out one day and I got to looking at my own career. When you're having fun is when your creativity is the best.

What role does commitment to short and long-term goals affect success as a hit songwriter?

The short-term goal is to wake up every day and see what happens that day. You must be present to win, so you gotta get up and believe that today is the day I might have that magic song. I always think I only need that one song—the one song that everyone will love. Of course, the long-term goal is to have a career as a songwriter and to keep writing songs-persevere and have fun while you're doing it. If you aren't having fun, then it won't be long-term. You have to see yourself successful. You have to look at yourself and say, by golly, I can do this, and I'm going to create something that people love. If you like it and you're picky enough, and you're writing things you love, eventually someone else will love it, too.

Do you believe that learning from failures and rejections help in becoming a hit songwriter? Please elaborate.

Sure. There is a fine line between failure and rejection. Lots of times when you're rejected it doesn't mean you're a failure. If you fail, it doesn't always mean you weren't good enough. That's kind of the thick-skinned thing. Early on you learn maybe why you failed or why a song wasn't good enough. I think it's important for an aspiring songwriter to know where the bar is. I was fortunate to have that in me, whatever that is, to realize that a year into being in town, my songs really weren't good enough. I realized they needed to get better. I saw that and knew where the bar was to get my songs on records. Unfortunately, once you start ringing the bell and reaching the bar, that doesn't mean your songs are going to end up on a record. That's the frustrating part of the music business. Just part of it.

Interview with Songwriter **Wil Nance**

Do you feel like being obsessive and persistent with writing help in becoming a successful, hit songwriter? If so, how?

Definitely. You have to keep trying to write "that song." The perfect example, we used to write with paper and pencil, before laptops and all that came into play. I had a laundry basket full of writing, probably 20 years' worth of writing. I remember digging through that basket, and I had a song that Brad Paisley did called, "She's Everything," and I found in that laundry basket at least 7,8,9, 10 times of trying to write that song, but really didn't write that song. I was trying to write that song but I really just writing a bunch of stuff to get to that song. That's persistence. You have to keep writing and keep trying to say something in a different way. You have to be as interesting as you can. Must write a lot of songs.

Do you think taking risks in your career has helped you become successful? If so, how?

It's a risk just to be a songwriter. It's a risk to pack up and move to Nashville. I definitely think that if I hadn't taken a risk, I wouldn't have gone down the path I went. I was here 8 ½ years before I got a cut of any significance. It's always risky. If you don't take a risk, you'll never know. It's risky not to take a risk. Comes back to perseverance—if you're going to take the risk, you have to persevere. For how long, that's up to the individual.

Do you believe having a positive mental attitude, being optimistic, and possessing a strong self-esteem play a major role in success? If so, how?

Yes. That's back to faith and hope. In my case, it's a Godly thing. You have to believe in yourself, and there is a purpose. You have to see yourself being successful, and you must have a positive attitude. Number one, no one really wants to be around someone who is negative. Even though I've seen some negative people be successful, but for the most part, they had the inner thing where they believe it's going to happen. You have to be a believer, all around. Basically, if you don't believe in yourself, no one will.

Does being a doer and not a talker help in becoming successful? If so, how?

You can't just be talker. You actually have to do it. I think it was Fred Foster that once said, if you have to tell me how great the song is, then it's probably not that great of a song. I'm not sure if that's the same thing but, just do it. Just write the song. People talk, talk, talk but if they don't do it, what's the point. You know since I've been in Nashville, I bet I've written 3000 songs. You have to do something a lot to get good at it. The more you do it, the better you get.

Does being a visionary or a dreamer help artists become successful? If so, how?

Yes. You have to be a dreamer to be in this business. To be any kind of artist, you have to be a dreamer and believe something is going to happen. It's a dream. Sometimes the dream doesn't end up the way you want it to, but you definitely have to be a dreamer.

Do you think overall personality contributes to the success of a songwriter? If so, how?

Yes, it contributes, but there are all types of personalities in songwriting. Some are more subdued, withdrawn, and then there is the opposite-more outgoing, talk more. I met people of all types of personalities that were hit songwriters. You know, sometimes the type of personality portrays the styles of songs you write. It takes all kinds of songs to make the world go around.

Do you feel patience and practice play a role in the creation of a hit songwriter? How?

You definitely have to have patience because things move very slow around here. It's like hurry up and wait. You wait and wait to get a good idea, wait to learn how to write the idea, then you wait to see if it gets recorded...and then if it gets recorded, you wait to see if it's a single; if it's a single, you have to wait 9 months for the money. Yes, patience is a big virtue, grasshopper. Practice makes perfect. The more you do something, the better you get. The more songs you have, the better songs you're going to have. You never know what will happen. You might go 8 months and not write one single song, and one day you'll write that big song.

How much prioritizing your life from day-to-day helps you become successful? If so, how?

I think your priority is to write as much as possible, but I also know you could burn yourself out. I've gotten the same amount of song ideas painting a wall as I did sitting down trying to write a song. Matter of fact, a lot of my ideas have either been driving down the road or watching TV; taking time out to watch a movie. You gotta live to be able to write songs; you can't just write songs. If you're a decent writer, you're writing about life.

Do you continue to learn all you can about your profession? If so, how?

I'm always trying to write that next thing or something that breaks new ground. I'm always listening and studying. If a songwriter gets really hot, I'll listen to 7 or 8 of their songs and try to see what they are doing. The way music evolves today—the same type of song isn't getting cut that was getting cut 25 years ago. If you are going to stay in the business, you have to keep learning. You have to keep studying songwriters, new and old. Every day you have to get up and ask yourself, what am I going to learn today. Then there is the writing part. I think every songwriter should learn some business. How the money is split up—you have to know that stuff to keep an eye on your own business.

In any part of your life, has self-discipline played a major role in helping become successful? If so, how?

I've never been a quitter. You have to be self-disciplined to get up every day and do it over and over and over again. I can't tell you how many times, I've been here 31 years; I can't tell you how many times I've driven to Music Row and back. You have to be self-disciplined. I believe any songwriter will tell you that. It's a job.

Is there any factor, trait, or ingredient we may have omitted that helps in becoming a successful, hit songwriter?

You always have to have your antenna up. You always have to be looking for ideas. You have to be eaten up with it. You have to be constantly thinking about songwriting. I probably did it more when I was younger than I do now, but that's all I thought about when I was around 35 years old. I was constantly looking for that next idea, searching for that hook. You have to be a songwriter, not a song maker-upper. Look around you and write songs about what you see. What you are seeing, someone else is seeing it too, and that's the trick. You want to write something that everyone can relate to. You really have to think about that when you are writing and have fun. If it ain't no fun, then it ain't no fun!

Do you believe a hit songwriter is born or made? Why?

Interesting question. I think songwriting is half craft and half talent. I don't think anybody is born a songwriter, I think the talent is there, but I think once they learn how to craft the song, then they are miles above everyone else. They have the God-given talent. Mel Tillis comes to mind. He wrote two or three hit songs, and he said he had no idea what he had done. I think in that case he had a knack for writing catchy things and structure was out the window. It wasn't so much about the craft; it was about what sounds goods. There's another song by Jessie Coulter to was married to Waylon Jennings who wrote a song called, "I'm Not Lisa." If you listen to that song, you can kind of tell there is no structure, there is a structure there, but it goes wherever and it's brilliant. That's because she had that songwriting chip in her that made her be able to do that. I don't think everyone has that. I think anyone can learn to write songs, but that doesn't necessarily mean they will write great ones. Tom Petty said something like, "Everyone can do it, but not everyone can do it well."

Do you believe talent is a gift or is it earned? Explain your thoughts.

I think it's a gift, but I also think it's earned. No one really knows what their potential is until you develop is. The potential is the talent. Someone may be super talented, but they never reached their potential. That's where practice and perseverance, the learning, drive, and the want to comes in. You have to really want it.

Do you believe that talent comes from within? If so, is it how they process stimuli in life?

It's how you process. I think a great writer can see what everyone else is seeing, but they explain it in a profound way, but everyone still gets it. I always look at writing like, if I have an idea and I want to get it to the masses, I'm starting with a blank canvass. I always say, I'm trying to paint of a tree, and I'm trying to make it as simple as I can without being boring. It has to be interesting but where my eight-year-old daughter will get it when she hears it. It's hard to explain what I'm after and I don't reach it every day. I kind of know what I'm after and when it's all said and done, I know when I think it's right. A lot goes into it; the right words and music, the right structure—to reach that thing, where that song is the best it's going to get. I'll say this, some of the of the time; we don't what we are doing. It's all a slip of a paint brush.

What is talent?

I think talent is a God-given thing. It's funny; I didn't pick up a fiddle till later in life—I always thought talent was part of--you take a fiddler that has been playing all their life—part of talent is God-given, but a lot of it is the want to. You take a child at 5,6,7 and they have the desire to want to play that instrument, granted there are different levels of talent, but if you get started on something that young and you like doing it and you're having fun—you're going to be really good at it by the time you're 20 years old. It's like teaching a five-year-old to read and write and then teaching a four-year-old. The five-year-old is going to learn it just like that, but the four-year-old might struggle. Then there are the prodigies, that's God. They have super talent. I believe we are all born with talents. There are better songwriters than others, but that doesn't mean that someone with half the talent won't write a song just as great as the more talented writer.

Do you believe self-criticism helps or harms the success of a hit songwriter? Explain.

It helps. It only harms you if you let it. I think we have all been there when it hurts us. I think listening to others is good but when it comes to something like that, but if you really believe in something and you know where the bar is; you're ringing the bell with that piece of work—you have to believe in what you do. No matter what anyone says—there will always be that person that doesn't like what you do. If you really believe in something, I say go with it. You have to be careful with the criticism.

Do you believe hit songwriters are more attuned to what is going on and happening around them than others? Please elaborate.

Yay and nay. I do believe that there are some guys in town that are "flavor of the month." I think I'm pretty attuned to what's going on but when you are "flavor of the month" and everyone is cutting your songs, I think there is a formula they get onto, and it works for them. I could do the same formula but because I'm not "flavor of the month," I might not get a cut. These guys are very attuned to what's going on, and every day they are writing songs that are ringing that bell, and it sounds like something on the radio. You have to be attuned to what is going on; you can't be oblivious. I can't write the same song I wrote 25 years ago. Music evolves, and I have to try to write something that will work for today.

Do you believe inspiration is a state of mind and could it be a major factor in the creation of a hit songwriter? Why?

I believe inspiration is a state of mind. I go in spurts with ideas. Somedays everything sounds like a song and somedays, nothing sounds like a song. There are days when you could tell me the best idea in the world, and I would think it sounds like a song and other days, you could tell me the worst idea, and I would write it with you. It's definitely a state of mind. You have to remember that as well when you are pitching songs. Listening is a state of mind. One day your song will hit a person emotionally, and the next day they won't get it at all. We are human beings. Day to day we are in different moods. One day we'll love something and the next we won't like it at all. That's why I pitch the same songs to the same people a few times; you never know if they will like it.

Do you believe having empathy helps in becoming a hit songwriter? Explain.

I think all great songwriters have a sensitive side where they understand what others are going through, whether it is happy or sad. It's emotions; sad or romantic--empathy definitely helps.

From left to right: Recording artist, **Brad Paisley**; hit songwriter, **Wil Nance** and his wife, Holly.

Chapter Eighteen:

Interview with Songwriter **Tony Conniff**

Songwriter, artist, producer, songwriting coach and teacher, **Tony Conniff**

Tony Conniff is a songwriter, artist, producer, songwriting coach and teacher based in New York City. He has released two albums ('Let It Drown Me' in 2016 and 'Tight Leash' in 2018), has produced numerous other artists at his studio, and is the owner of Tony Conniff Songwriting Workshops. He also writes a weekly blog on songwriting at www.tonyconniff.com/blog/.

Do you believe drive, passion, and stamina (energy level) play a major role in helping a person to become a successful hit songwriter?

Yes. The world is full of people who are musically talented and have a gift for songwriting. Drive, passion, and endurance is what makes the difference between those who will create a career in the music business and those who won't.

Do you think work ethic plays a vital part in becoming a hit songwriter? If so, how?

Yes. Since in songwriting you're basically self-employed, you're likely to fail without consistent application. The competition is too tough and hard working. 'Consistent application' varies; writers have their own work methods, routines, schedules, and non-schedules. Whatever works...but you have to get the job(s) done; you have to produce.

How much does faith and belief in one's abilities help in becoming a hit songwriter?

It's important, of course. But perhaps even more important is faith in one's ability to learn and to improve.

How much of focus to detail and perfection helps make a hit songwriter?

Although there are plenty of hit songs where this may not have been the case, I think it's hard to be consistently excellent and successful at anything challenging without an obsessive attention to the fine points. (Which doesn't mean there isn't a time to let go and move on.)

What role does commitment to short and long-term goals affect success as a hit songwriter?

I think this is very helpful, but it's hard to generalize.

Do you believe that learning from failures and rejections help in becoming a hit songwriter? Please elaborate.

As with anything, this is the case. To use a boxing metaphor, if you get knocked down, even if you need some recovery time, you have to get back up and learn from your mistakes if you want to fight-and-win-another day.

Do you feel like being obsessive and persistent with writing help in becoming a successful hit songwriter? If so, how

See #4!

Do you think taking risks in your career has helped you become successful? If so, how?

I believe in an incremental approach, in building something, which is usually a gradual process. So, I'd call that a calculated risk. Just being a songwriter is in itself an enormous risk (and pleasure)!

Do you believe having a positive mental attitude, being optimistic, and possessing strong self-esteem play a major role in success? If so, how?

Yes... but many people with low self-esteem and an enormous amount of self-doubt succeed. You just have to keep plugging... and believing, if not in yourself, then in your talent, and that something good might happen if you stick with it. Music is a business where 'many are called, few are chosen.' So, you usually have to put in a lot of time (and work) to even have the chance of being one of the ones who find success.

Does being a doer and not a talker help in becoming successful? If so, how?

Certainly, the 'sizzle' is helpful, especially in sales, but ultimately, it's the 'steak,' the substance, that matters. If you don't walk it like you talk it, you'll be exposed soon enough.

Does being a visionary or a dreamer help artists become successful? If so, how?

Yes. But you can't fake this or will it. And you don't always know in advance who the visionaries will turn out to be and if you might be one of them. There can be a lot of self-delusion here (but that's show business!)

Do you think overall personality contributes to the success of a songwriter? If so, how?

Yes. Being a basically friendly person with integrity makes a big difference, particularly in the long run. It's a networking business; it's a relatively small world. People skills, both with collaborators and business people, are really helpful, even vital. That said, people with every kind of personality succeed as songwriters. There's definitely no 'type'; as they say, it takes all kinds.

Do you feel patience and practice play a role in the creation of a hit songwriter?

Indisputably. Patience - sadly, things move at their own pace, usually not at mine. Practice - you have to write a LOT of songs to end up with a bunch of good ones, some of which may even become hits.

How much prioritizing your life from day-to-day helps you become successful?

I think this is very important. I have to keep my eye, however imperfectly, on the big goals, so they don't get washed away by the day-to-day minutiae of life.

Do you continue to learn all you can about your profession? If so, how?

I try. I write regularly. I present and go to songwriting-related events. I perform and record and release albums of new material. I play, study, and analyze other writers' songs that I love or interest me. I've been writing a weekly songwriting blog for

Interview with Songwriter **Tony Conniff**

6 years, which helps me stay focused on learning new things and passing them on to other songwriters (www.tonyconniff/blog/).

In any part of your life, has self-discipline played a major role in helping become successful? If so, how?

I prefer to think of it as 'willingness to work' rather than 'you have to work' (I don't respond well to being ordered around, even by myself). Unless I really do have to get it done, as with a deadline. So yes, self-discipline is critical. But even people with limited self-discipline can find ways of doing work that they love and challenging... as long as they don't wait around to 'feel like it.'

Is there any factor, trait, or ingredient we may have omitted that helps in becoming a successful, hit songwriter?

Drive, talent, stubborn commitment, ability and willingness to learn. Being a part of a songwriting community and trying to connect with and help others in it is important too. And last but far from least, love of songs and songwriting.

Do you believe a hit songwriter is born or made? Explain your thoughts.

Made. Talent is given, but I don't know of any people who were born hit songwriters.

Do you believe talent is a gift or is it earned? Explain your thoughts.

It's a gift. What you do with it is earned.

Do you believe that talent comes from within? If so, is it how they process stimuli in life?

I pass on this one.

What is talent?
What you start with.

Do you believe self-criticism helps or harms the success of a hit songwriter?

It's crucial that, without being self-destructive, a songwriter never be too satisfied with their own work, and to believe that it can always be better. This is simple humility in the face of something - music and songs - much larger than any one of us.

Do you believe hit songwriters are more attuned to what is going on and happening around them than others?

Generally speaking, yes. A writer may not be tuned in personally, but on an artistic level, you need to be. Hit songs are of their time; so usually, the writers of them must be part of their times too.

Do you believe inspiration is a state of mind, and could it be a major factor in the creation of a hit songwriter? Why?

I don't know if I'd call it a 'state of mind,' but I think songwriters need to be tuned in to their personal 'songwriting channel.' If you're not tuned in, you miss what's being broadcast to you.

Do you believe having empathy helps in becoming a hit songwriter? Explain.

I believe it can be. Empathy for others and for yourself. You have to be able to feel something to write it. The more open you are to feelings, yours and others, and to trying to understand them, the more material you have to write abo

Chapter Nineteen:

Interview with Songwriter **Thornton Cline**

Author and songwriter, **Thornton Cline**

Ever since his mother signed him up for piano lessons, Thornton Cline has been writing non-stop. With over 1,000 published songs, 150 recorded songs, twenty-six adult, YA and children's books published, Thornton Cline has been nominated multiple times for Grammy and Dove Awards. Cline has been honored with "Songwriter of the Year" twice-in-a-row and received a platinum-certified award for sales of over one million album units in Europe. He won the first place Maxy Literary Award 2017 for "Children's Young Adult Book," and has had his songs recorded by Engelbert Humperdinck, Gloria Gaynor, Rebecca Holden, Gary Puckett, Tim Murphy, Ray Peterson, Tammy Trent, Billy, and Sarah Gaines, Matt Newton among others. Many of Cline's tunes have appeared in the top of the charts.

Cline continues to mentor, teach and inspire aspiring authors and songwriters all around the world as CEO/president of his publishing company, Clinetel Music. He is a faculty member of Cumberland University, Sumner Academy and Welch College.

Do you believe drive, passion, and stamina (energy level) play a major role in helping a person to become a successful hit songwriter?

Yes, I believe drive and passion are essential to becoming a successful hit songwriter. The songwriting business is a 24/7 career. There is no room for "every now and then writers," "part-time writers," "talkers" or "dreamers." If you are a "low-energy" person, the songwriting business is not for you. Sure, balance is important, and it helps to create inspiration and a muse for writing, but it's the drive and the passion that will help you rise above the competition. Songwriting isn't just about writing all day long, seven-days-a-week, it is also about demoing, pitching, networking, co-writing, and dealing with the paperwork business side of the industry. Many times, this business can be exhausting where songwriters get little or no sleep. You can be mega-talented or gifted in songwriting, but without the drive or passion, you won't get very far. You must be passionate about songwriting 24/7 even if you don't make any money out of it.

Do you think work ethic plays a vital part in becoming a hit songwriter? If so, how?

Yes, work ethic is an essential trait to possess to achieve success in anything. I believe you can learn it. My parents instilled in me work ethic and taught me the value of hard work at the age of five. I observed their discipline, values and hard work. Unfortunately, I have noticed some people in the younger generations are not into hard work and have perhaps never been taught work ethic. That is a shame since hard work combined with talent and gifts can equate with major successes provided the opportunities come along.

How much does faith and belief in one's abilities help in becoming a hit songwriter?

Faith and belief in yourself and your abilities are everything. People can tell if you really believe in yourself. And if you have complete confidence in yourself, others will be confident in you also. But I don't just believe in myself. I have a strong faith and belief in people and in God. There are co-writers, publishers, producers, and artists I have become friends with. I believe in their abilities, talent, and gifts. I have faith that working together with them will produce successful results and that I am not wasting my time. I trust God will help me develop my gifts and talents to the highest level possible provided I work hard at using my gifts. I also have faith God will guide my pathway in life and place opportunities and the people I'm supposed to work with along the way.

How much of focus to detail and perfection helps make a hit songwriter?

Detail and perfection are so important in hit songwriting, particularly in the editing process. The NSAI (Nashville Songwriters Association International) motto, "it all begins with a song" is so true. Inspiration hits you, you write a brilliant song with a hit idea, and then it's time to perfect it through editing. So many times, songwriters make the mistake of rushing the writing process. I have been guilty of being so excited about a song I wrote, I was ready to demo and pitch it. But now I learn not to rush the process. Take your time, live with the song and put it away for a while, then come back to it with new, fresh ears as if you were a stranger listening the song for the first time. Once I start the editing process, I tweak the melody, harmony, production, and lyrics to the way my instinct tells me to. I suppose it is possible to overthink or overwrite a song so that it has lost its mojo, but I believe you will know instinctively if you are helping your song climb to a new level or if you are driving it into the ground.

What role does commitment to short and long-term goals affect success as a hit songwriter?

Commitment and patience are so important. It's something some of the younger generation is lacking. Each January, I start the year by writing down my short and long-term goals. I make a written contract with myself and commit my goals to God with the belief that I will achieve. I review my goals each year and make note of the goals I have achieved and the ones I have fallen short of. I realize some goals take longer than others. That is why I remain patient and steady, never giving up. Many hit producers, artists, and songwriters say Nashville is a seven to 10-year-town as far as making it in the music business. I am sure Los Angeles, New York, and London are similar in the number of years it takes to succeed. Many songwriters quit too soon. If they had only stayed a few more years or so, they would have experienced their first hit. It's sad how they missed out on success because they didn't hang in there long enough.

Do you believe that learning from failures and rejections help in becoming a hit songwriter? Please elaborate.

Yes, learning from failures and rejections can be valuable to success. I prefer not to use the words "failures" and "rejections." I think of them as a process of elimination taking me one step closer to success. It's the same thinking process Thomas Edison used when it took him hundreds of times to finally invent the light bulb. Edison never thought of the words, "rejections" or "failures." He believed those passes were stepping stones which led him to success. My first hit song, "Love is the Reason" was turned down 124 times before two major, legendary artists recorded it. My song went on to be recorded 10 times and is still being recorded today. It has reached platinum status in Germany and helped me to be named "Songwriter of the Year" twice in a row. Whenever someone turns down one of my songs, I feel like the song wasn't right for them and that it was their loss for not recording it. I always feel like someone will get it and will record the song even if it is years from now. I have had 20-year-old songs recorded, and they have been successful. Perhaps the time or artist at the time weren't meant for the song, or the song was ahead of its time.

Do you feel like being obsessive and persistent with writing help in becoming a successful hit songwriter? If so, how?

Yes, being obsessed and persistent are key traits to becoming a successful hit songwriter. Many people lack those traits today. You have to pitch your song a million times if you have to. As mentioned in the previous answer, I pitched my song 124 times before it was cut ten times. I believe in following up with people persistently without being obnoxious. That is another practice many younger-generation people fail to apply. I will wear a new song out when I edit and rewrite, so the song is perfect. I always trust my instincts to make sure I am elevating my new song to a whole new level and standard. Unfortunately, some songs you hear on the radio or on Spotify don't seem to have been polished. It doesn't matter if there are two or 13 writers, I still hear some of the same, tired, worn-out productions, riffs, melodies, chords, and trite, non-creative lyrics. It is almost as if songs are being cloned and manufactured on an assembly line. I realize art and music are subjective. But you've got to ask yourself, "how in the world did some of the songs make it to the top 10?" Then again, every once-in-awhile you hear an amazing, different- kind-of song and it is a breath of fresh air.

Do you think taking risks in your career has helped you become successful? If so, how?

Yes, taking risks have helped me to succeed. But not every risk taken has resulted in success. I have hired up-and-coming new artists to demo some of my songs and little did I know I was pitching my songs to them. I have had cuts as a result of that practice. Sometimes, when I've met an artist or producer for the first time, I will ask them if I can pitch my songs. Some have led to successes while others have led to the run-around. Choosing to become a songwriter is risky. But I believe you must be willing to risk it all as a writer.

Do you believe having a positive mental attitude, being optimistic, and possessing strong self-esteem play a major role in success? If so, how?

Yes, you must act like you know what you're doing even if you don't. That attitude and philosophy worked for Steven Spielberg, and I am sure it has worked for many artists, producers, and songwriters. Call it dishonest, but I call it confidence and, optimism. If you exhibit a positive mental attitude, many people will believe in, you and follow you.

Does being a doer and not a talker help in becoming successful? If so, how?

Yes. Being a doer is everything. I don't mean to sound rude or judgmental, but I get so sick and tired of running into talkers. The world is full of dreamers, mediocrity, and talkers. They all sound alike with their excuses, blaming and reasons for why they can't do something. When I finally get to meet and work with a doer, it is so refreshing because by the mere act of doing they are telling me they are serious, and I can count on working with them. They are not flaking.

Does being a visionary or a dreamer help artists become successful? If so, how?

Yes, it helps to visualize the act of success. But a dream is only a dream until you write it down, commit to it, and work hard at achieving that dream. Productive dreaming can be very useful. I have written entire songs and books after waking up from dreams. I can remember every detail of my dreams and have applied those details to my songs and books. Since I was very young, I have seen the "successful" me in my mind accomplishing goals I never thought were achievable.

Do you think overall personality contributes to the success of a songwriter? If so, how?

Yes, I believe you can tell if an introvert or extrovert wrote a particular song by the way feelings are portrayed and projected. The personality of a songwriter is what can help to make a song special or unique. Of course, when you're co-writing all co-writers need to get along. It is difficult or impossible to work with some narcissistic, selfish and controlling songwriters. It is much easier to work with writers who are flexible, agreeable, and who leave their egos at the door.

Do you feel patience and practice play a role in the creation of a hit songwriter?

Yes, patience is so necessary with songwriting. The songwriting business is one of those "hurry-up-and-wait" businesses. Artists, producers, publishers and record companies don't seem to be in a rush to get business done. They take their sweet time. The best thing you can do while waiting for a hold, a decision on a song, or a cut is to practice your craft and inspiration hard. Write and write, and write with artists, producers, and other songwriters. Practice doesn't always make perfect, but perfect practice makes perfect. Always write up with someone more advanced and skilled than you are so you are always improving and not stuck in practicing the same-old writing habits. Learn new tricks and skills.

How much prioritizing your life from day-to-day helps you become successful?

You must be a dedicated, committed songwriter by writing every day or else you have no right to call yourself a songwriter. I know people who call themselves songwriters but only write one or two songs a year if best. They dream of being writers and have even convinced themselves in their minds they are songwriters. They are dreamers, talkers and possibly recreational songwriters. You have to be willing to block off a certain amount of time every day including weekends to writing songs. And then you must be willing set to aside regular time to network, demo and pitch songs, that is if you are truly serious about songwriting. You can't just dabble in it from time-to-time and expect to be successful at it. It's either all or nothing.

Do you continue to learn all you can about your profession? If so, how?

Yes, I am constantly learning. I learn a lot from writing with other artists, songwriters, and producers. When I had a five-year-songwriting deal with It's A Good Thing Publishing/Gatlin Brothers music, I wrote with every songwriter and artist in Nashville. I learned something from each person in the over 400 songs I wrote and applied that knowledge to my own songwriting. I continue to learn all I can by attending songwriting conferences and workshops, The ASCAP Expos, the Taxi conferences, and the winter/summer NAMM shows are great places to continue.

In any part of your life, has self-discipline played a major role in helping become successful? If so, how?

Yes, self-discipline is the key to it all in success. I learned self-discipline at the early age of five when my mother signed me up for piano lessons. I studied piano and violin, regularly attended orchestra practices, gave recitals, practiced one-to-three hours-a-day. My musical studies taught me how to manage time and not waste it, how to schedule my day, how to be structured, how to set goals and achieve them, and how to be on time for appointments. I often practiced even when I didn't feel like it. I knew that if I didn't practice, I would be embarrassed or humiliated by playing poorly in an audition, recital or performance. I also learned how to pace myself like a runner does not to tire too early. Also, I had to work for everything I received. There were no entitlements. I earned everything. While others in high school were given their first car, I had bought my first with the money I had saved; money from mowing lawns, delivering papers, taking odd jobs and selling everything legally I could get my hands on. The self-discipline I have learned from my childhood days has served me well in everything I do today, not just in music but life in general. I am thankful to my parents for not giving me handouts. Everything I have worked for has meant something.

Is there any factor, trait, or ingredient we may have omitted that helps in becoming a successful, hit songwriter?

Yes, brilliant hit songs can be written in five minutes or can take days, weeks or months to create. Still, even with quickly-written-songs, you must edit and perfect. One ingredient we didn't touch on is the act of kindness. I believe as a songwriter and a decent human being, we must practice the art of kindness and show thoughtful manners to others. I believe those acts go a long way in a cold and distant world. It makes us stand out from the crowd. That is another ingredient we didn't touch on—trying to be different and to rise above the noise. Too many songwriters and artists believe if they sound or write like the last hit artist or songwriter they will succeed. Some do succeed with that approach, but with most, their success is a fleeting thing. Dare to be different with your writing and singing. Stand out of the crowd. Be the leader others follow. Don't follow trends but set them. The world doesn't need another Katy Perry, Garth Brooks or Taylor Swift. The world already has their talents. Be yourself unique, original self.

Do you believe a hit songwriter is born or made? Explain your thoughts.

I believe you can be born a hit songwriter and it comes naturally to you. At the same time, I believe a songwriter can become talented by hard work and thousands of hours of practice and effort. The premise of "The Talent Code" is that you can become a talented, master of something if you practice a skill for at least 10,000 hours.

Do you believe talent is a gift or is it earned? Explain your thoughts.

I believe talent is earned by countless hours of hard work and learning. "The Talent Code" is a much-researched book which teaches that talent is learned by practicing a skill for at least 10,000 hours. A songwriter has to be dedicated and committed to practicing his or her craft for at least 10,000 hours to become a master or the best. I believe talent is NOT a gift. I believe a gift comes from above and within. I believe people are given gifts when they are born. An example would be Mozart. While Mozart wasn't a songwriter like we know today, he was a genius composer and did write some lyrics to operas and songs. Mozart started writing music at the early age of three. There is no way Mozart could have practiced his writing for 10,000 hours at that early age. I believe gifts are natural and are second-nature to the gifted. There are some very gifted songwriters who write both lyrics and melodies easily, and their songs are created with little or no effort. Songs come naturally to them, and they are generally prolific. But a talented or gifted songwriter still must work hard with commitment, or it will all be a wasted talent or gift.

Do you believe that talent comes from within? If so, is it how they process stimuli in life?

I believe gifts come from above and within. Talent is earned by hard work of constant practice of at 10,000 hours or more. That is why many say it takes seven to 10 years to become a hit songwriter. If a songwriter writes or co-writes eight-hours-a-day, five days a week for one year, the songwriter has written or practiced for 2000 hours, Now multiply that number by seven to 10 years, and you arrive at 14,000 to 20,000 hours. If the songwriter maintained that a yearly number of hours for five years, the writer would have written at least 10,000 hours. I believe with that kind of talent; a songwriter would be very sensitive and attuned to the environment around him or her. That songwriter should be able to process stimuli masterfully.

What is talent?

Talent is a skill learned and mastered to a high level. It reflects the personality, creativity, and knowledge of a person.

Do you believe self-criticism helps or harms the success of a hit songwriter?

Constructive self-criticism helps the songwriter to attain success, provided the songwriter isn't wearing his or her feelings on his or her sleeve and doesn't take it personally.

Do you believe hit songwriters are more attuned to what is going on and happening around them than others?

Yes, but they see the picture differently than others. They may even become emotional or analytical about a situation happening around them. They may also see another point of view or angle to the story.

Do you believe inspiration is a state of mind, and could it be a major factor in the creation of a hit songwriter? Why?

Inspiration can be a state of mind like being hypnotized or being in a trance. I believe inspiration is different for each person. Sometimes a word or phrase someone has said can trigger inspiration. Sometimes a major high or low emotionally can give me inspiration. The change in the weather, nature or environment can affect me. However, it happens to each writer; it can be a huge factor in creating a hit song.

Do you believe having empathy helps in becoming a hit songwriter? Explain.

Empathy plays a large part in successful songwriting. You try to step inside someone's mind, heart or soul and feel the emotion someone is feeling. Then you write your song in such a way that everyone can feel or relate with that emotion universally. It is gratifying to know millions of people are connecting with that same feeling you felt from the empathy for someone.

Chapter Twenty:

Interview with Songwriter **Lacie Carpenter**

Author/Artist/Songwriter, and
Award-Winning Instrumentalist, **Lacie Carpenter**

Hailing from Texas and graduating from Stephen F. Austin University with her degree in Music Education/ specialization in Violin Performance and an MS in Psychology--Lacie teaches private lessons in many musical genres, writing courses, and is an adjunct psychology professor. She performs globally with other artists and her one-woman show. With her 4-string acoustic violin and her 7-string fretted, Mark Wood Viper (The Beast,) and her eclectic vocal stylings—from concert halls to house concerts…she puts on quite the show. She has performed internationally with 9 symphonies, chamber orchestras, choirs, symphonic bands, and solo acts. Lacie studied with Dr. Jennifer Dalmas, Dr. Isidor Saslav and Dr. Jane Saber. For 7 years, she built orchestra programs in Texas before moving to Nashville, TN to pursue her many ambitions. Lacie is an active songwriter, author, session player, arranger, blogger, and church choir member.

She is the winner of 12 East Texas Music Awards, but the ones she is most proud of are Fiddler Of The Year 2012-2014, 2016 and 2017. In 2015, Lacie was awarded ETX Bluegrass Act of the Year.

Lacie has been able to grace the stage with greats such as Mark O'Connor, Mark Wood, Judy Hyman, Jonna Fitzgerald, Bruce Molsky, Isidor Saslav, and Jimmy Fortune. Her first album, "Nothing is Real," debuted in October 2018 and was produced by Wayne Moss. She is also the fiddler for Jerry Vandiver. Her first novel, AKA which she co-wrote with Thornton Cline, hit the shelves early 2019.

Do you believe drive, passion, and stamina (energy level) play a major role in helping a person to become a successful hit songwriter? If so, how?

Absolutely! I believe that if someone has the drive and passion for anything, they will stop at nothing to get where they want to be. You have to have this everlasting fire to keep at songwriting-it isn't an easy job. To write from a vulnerable state, it takes a lot of stamina. You must ask very difficult questions to yourself while writing, and occasionally, that becomes an energy vampire. Be aware of your energy levels and know when you need to take a break. Without passion and a drive for songwriting—really anything you want to do in life; you won't make it.

Do you think work ethic plays a vital part in becoming a hit songwriter? If so, how?

Yes. There are days when all I do is write and other days, practicing for shows. Every day, I start with prayer, exercise, coffee, writing and practicing. I know there are days when I won't get anything written because I'm working on new material for a show. Same when I'm on a roll writing. I believe, that in order to achieve greatness and success, one must work hard. Even when success is thrust upon someone; in order to keep that status of success, they have to keep working.

How much does faith and belief in one's abilities help in becoming a hit songwriter? If so, how?

This business isn't for the faint-hearted. If you don't believe in yourself first; who will? Now, there is a fine line between faith in yourself and over-confidence—narcissism... whatever you want to call it. You also have to have faith that your hard work will pay off, even though it feels like it won't. Faith is crucial. There is this hopefulness that lives inside you when you have constant faith. Without belief and faith, the business can eat you up alive.

How much of focus to detail and perfection helps make a hit songwriter?

Songwriting is a craft and a skill. Careful attention to how you build and perfect that song is important—just like building a house. You have to pay attention to wording---the layers and structure. Throwing words onto a piece of paper isn't going to get you a song, much less a hit song. Know what you want to say then piece it together focusing on important words, structure, the story, etc. Some songs come to me quickly. The structure, the words, the melody, and chords are already in my head. Other times, the majority of the song comes then I have to work and mold it like a piece of clay.

What role does commitment to short and long-term goals affect success as a hit songwriter?

To be honest, I'm not a very goal-oriented person. However, I knew what I wanted to be when I was nine years old. I was committed to becoming a musician and songwriter when I saw Burt Bacharach. I shouted it out loud for the world to hear--the rest is hard work to get there. I set small, long-term goals. Mainly I think about where I want to perform, who I want to write a song for, who I want to work with. Then, I write it out and lastly, I say it out loud. To me, it's best if I say it to a person, I am comfortable sharing my emotions with. That way, they can help me keep accountable to those desires.

Do you believe that learning from failures and rejections help in becoming a hit songwriter? Please elaborate.

I think so. Failure means you tried. Without trying, then you would have never received an answer. Rejection doesn't mean you're bad at what you do--just not right for the job or the song isn't right for the artist. Failure shouldn't be looked down upon. There is this stigma that comes with that word that is terribly negative. Rejection hurts—not going to lie. Are you tough enough to work through the failure and rejection? Learn from it and grow within the craft of songwriting. Take a songwriting course at a university or find a mentor. Listen to music all the time—good, bad, and ugly. Learn and keep at it. There is another side of this though...if someone constantly has success and never fails or been rejected; the first time it happens; they will fall hard, and it might break them. Enjoy your struggle.

Do you feel like being obsessive and persistent with writing help in becoming a successful, hit songwriter? If so, how?

Yes. I've been obsessed with music and writing my entire life. I don't go a day without either. The more you do it, the better you get.

Do you think taking risks in your career has helped you become successful? If so, how?

I'm not a risk taker by nature. I prefer taking

calculated risks. I weigh my options then decide. However, everything you do is a risk. Driving, flying, speaking to someone you've respected for years and finally have the chance to meet... I can see where my risks have paid off. For instance, moving to Nashville was a huge risk. I had a great job building and teaching middle school orchestras, but I had this burning passion to constantly create and I wasn't able to while teaching majority of the day. I had to take a risk—a leap of faith and move to Nashville. I knew it was the right place for me. I can also see where not taking a risk and being careful about my leaps have protected me. I'm a spiritual person. Before I take a risk, I pray about it. Sometimes, instead of saying "taking risks," I say, I'm going to be bold. That way, whatever happens, happens and it was because I tried. If you are constantly careful and never bold—your answer will always be "no."

Do you believe having a positive mental attitude, being optimistic, and possessing strong self-esteem play a major role in success? If so, how?

100%. If you are negative, your whole body is affected. Your songs won't be any good and they will be the same over and over again. If you are optimistic, it can come with a great deal of pain. Use it. Write about it. If you don't have a strong self-esteem, people will run all over you. Be positive and humble—the world will open up and there will be no stopping you from success.

Does being a doer and not a talker help in becoming successful? If so, how?

I think talking about it helps but then strap on those boots and get to work. People want to see you working and busy people get hired more. If you want to become a hit songwriter, stop talking about it and do it. Write until you can't write any more for that day. Pitch your songs. If you're a singer/songwriter-record your songs even if it's a cell-phone demo; go to songwriter round and share your songs and see how people react. Do it.

Does being a visionary or a dreamer help artists become successful? If so, how?

I think we all start off as a dreamer. We visualize ourselves winning some big award and even go so far as writing our acceptance speech. If you do that, then you know how much work you have to do to get there. Visualizing and dreaming about what you want in life is great! Your dreams might take a different shape after a while and know that's okay. When you do so, it makes all those rejections and failures disappear. After those negative things disappear, success happens because you believe it will.

Do you think overall personality contributes to the success of a songwriter? If so, how?

Sometimes. There are very successful people in this world that aren't the nicest. However, I know that people prefer to work with those who are pleasant. If you are nice and work hard, you will build up a good reputation. With that good reputation, people will talk and word will get out. Success happens when there is a good mixture of hard work, dedication, and a solid team. You cannot do this alone even if you feel like you can.

Do you feel patience and practice play a role in the creation of a hit songwriter? How?

Patience is a virtue that I don't have, but learning to have. It's difficult to have patience when writing a song, pitching a song, recording your creation, etc. You might think that once you write the song, the journey is over but it's just beginning. Practicing your craft is crucial. I come from a classical music background--you don't practice one day, everyone knows it. It's a harsh reality. Without practicing, there won't be success. Songwriting can be easy, but it can be very difficult at times; that's where your patience and practice comes in.

Interview with Songwriter **Lacie Carpenter**

How much prioritizing your life from day-to-day helps you become successful? If so, how?

A lot like goal-setting; I'm not very good at prioritizing. I allow inspiration to strike at moment's notice and in an instant; I'm buried in a sea of words and music. When that happens, I don't take phone calls or texts—my only priority is that song, piece of music, book, or something as simple as a set list for upcoming shows. I think that in order to have success in songwriting, you must consider the fact you will be constantly writing and sometimes that will affect the relationships that surround you. If you hold songwriting above a relationship; then they might say your priorities are off. But what do you want? Do you want to become a successful songwriter or go out with friends? If your friends don't understand your dreams and passions; then they weren't your true friends to begin with. Trust me--you will find your tribe of people that value your priorities and passions within this music world.

Do you continue to learn all you can about your profession? If so, how?

I'm constantly learning. I listen to every genre of music, take classes, and ask questions. People in songwriting/music business can be quite approachable, especially if you have the great desire to learn.

In any part of your life, has self-discipline played a major role in helping become successful? If so, how?

YES! I'm a trained classical violinist that decided to play other genres of music and write songs for a living. Self-discipline is very important for success. I remember going into my freshman year of college as a violin performance/music education major—the dean walked onto the stage in front of a large group of young musicians and said, "If you can do anything else; if you like anything else; if you don't see yourself as a professional in the music industry of some sort—get out." I'll never forget that. If you don't have this fire--this need to write or be in any part of the industry; your passion lies somewhere else. That's OKAY! You haven't failed. But if music is your deepest passion; then self-discipline is a necessity.

Is there any factor, trait, or ingredient we may have omitted that helps in becoming a successful, hit songwriter?

I think the willingness to go deeper than the surface in songwriting. Finding that vulnerability can be difficult, and we often don't want to go to that place mentally or emotionally. We certainly don't want to show our battle scars. Lots of songs are stories about pain, suffering, loss, grief, re-birth, happiness... Those stories hold truth within the words about that person—the writer and/or a character the song is about. We have to shed layers of ourselves in order to be the best in our craft.

Do you believe a hit songwriter is born or made? Why?

Both. You can be born with natural abilities, but you must work at those gifts to be truly successful.

Do you believe talent is a gift or is it earned? Explain your thoughts.

Both. Sometimes a gift is blessed to us from birth; other times that burning passion and self-discipline overrides the ones blessed with the gift. It's not enough to just be born with it-you gotta earn it, otherwise people who aren't naturally gifted will become more successful.

Do you believe that talent comes from within? If so, is it how they process stimuli in life?

I think talent comes from a lot of different sources. We are all gifted with something. We have to find what that talent is and work, work, work. Without processing what we go through on a daily basis and learning how to cope with the twists and turns life throws at us; then our talents won't reach the level of success they are meant to reach.

What is talent?

Difficult to say exactly. Talent is this entity that drives us mad sometimes. Some people think they have a certain talent but aren't willing to work for it. You might be born with a natural ability to write music, but success won't necessarily be thrust upon you. One thing is for certain; talent is God-given. After HE gives it to you, it's your choice what you do with it.

Do you believe self-criticism helps or harms the success of a hit songwriter? Explain.

I believe positive self-criticism helps but if you become too negative with your critiques then it becomes harmful. I think it's crucial to be objective. Even though our songs are like our children—we love them so much; we still have to stand back and ask very serious questions.

Do you believe hit songwriters are more attuned to what is going on and happening around them than others? Please elaborate.

I think so. Creative people, in general, are. We feel things a little deeper, see things in multiple different ways, and come up with multiple scenarios for everything. I don't watch television because it affects my writing. A swift change in weather can have a positive or negative effect on my writing. The power of kindness or sadness that I see or overhear can inspire me to write non-stop. I also have muses. These people are placed in my life by God and I must be aware of that.

Do you believe inspiration is a state of mind and could it be a major factor in the creation of a hit songwriter? Why?

Yes. As an artist, I write down ideas for shows, things people say in the grocery store, church, etc. that inspire me. Recently, I was having coffee with someone and BAM, they said something that became a song the next day. I know when I'm inspired and what will become a song. Sometimes it hits me so quickly that I don't have time to process it. Can I sit down and choose to write a song without some form of "inspiration?" Sure. I'm a songwriter. However, if we take a moment to sit in silence-everything that is surrounding us can be a form of inspiration. Every person, building, street…has a story; as songwriters, it's our job to tell the story.

Do you believe having empathy helps in becoming a hit songwriter? Explain.

I do. Empathy comes from deep within. You must care about others and the world. Creative people seem to have an extra amount of empathy that can be detrimental—unfortunately. Empathy is a wonderful quality to have and it will show within your music. Never allow the world to harden your feelings. If you do; soon you won't have feelings and you'll wonder, why you are not successful.

Chapter Twenty-One:

Interview with Executive Director of NSAI **Bart Herbison**

Executive Director of the Nashville Songwriters Association International, **Bart Herbison**

A Paris, Tenn., native, Bart Herbison worked as a reporter and spent 14 years in radio and as a correspondent for *The Nashville Banner* newspaper before joining the administration of former Tennessee Governor Ned McWherter as Deputy Director of Communications in 1987. Herbison joined the staff of U.S. Rep. Bob Clement (D-Nashville) in 1988 where he served as the Tennessee Congressman's Press Secretary, Campaign Manager, and Chief Tennessee Administrative Officer before leaving Capitol Hill for Music Row in 1997.

Herbison is Executive Director of the Nashville Songwriters Association International (NSAI), the world's largest not-for-profit songwriters trade organization and advocacy group dedicated to the songwriting profession. Established in 1967, NSAI's membership of nearly 5,000 spans the United States and many other countries. With more than 100 chapters, the association serves aspiring and professional songwriters in all genres of music. They also own The Bluebird Cafe in Nashville, Tennessee.

Under Herbison's leadership, NSAI gained prominence in the national legislative arena.

His accomplishments include:

- Adoption of the "Music Modernization Act" in 2018, the most important copyright law reform for songwriters in decades.
- Passage of the landmark "Songwriters Capital Gains Tax Equity Act" in 2006.
- Creation of the first-ever Group Copyright Infringement Insurance for songwriters and music publishers.
- Acquisition of the world-famous "Bluebird Café" in 2008
- Purchase of the "Music Mill" studios as NSAI headquarters in 2005.

In 2018 Herbison received two prestigious national honors for his songwriter advocacy work -- the "Industry Legacy Award" from the National Music Publishers Association (NMPA) and the "IP Champion's Award" from the U.S. Chamber of Commerce Global Innovation Policy Center.

Appearing in his first movie role, Herbison portrayed himself in the 2017 film "Wheeler" starring Stephen Dorff. He is also featured in the documentary "The Last Songwriter" released in 2018 and the upcoming documentary "It All Begins with A Song" where he serves as Executive Producer. He hosts the weekly video/print interview series "Story Behind the Song" appearing in *The Tennessean* and other Gannett newspapers.

Interview with Executive Director of NSAI **Bart Herbison**

Do you believe drive, passion, and stamina (energy level) play a major role in helping a person to become a successful hit songwriter?

I think passion and work ethic are part of the ingredients of success in any endeavor. And certainly, that's true with songwriting. The people that love it the most, that think about it all the time, that speak the language of songs, it's essential. And I don't think you can divorce that from success in this profession. Could you be a 'one-hit wonder' maybe as a songwriter or an artist? Of course. But you're not going to have a sustained career unless you're passionate about it, unless you work hard. I have to tell you I've heard so many stories and one that comes to mind is the song, "Live Like You Were Dying." And I think people could argue that is certainly one of the most, if not the most important modern country song. It was co-written by Craig Wiseman and Tim Nichols. Tim didn't feel good that day, or maybe it was Craig. I think it was Tim and they almost didn't get together that day. But they both have a work ethic, and they said, "you know, we're going to get together. We're going to write the song." And it became something that has moved lives across the planet. So yes, passion and work ethic are essential if you want to be a successful songwriter, especially over the long term.

Do you think work ethic plays a vital part in becoming a hit songwriter? If so, how?

Look, people want to know the secret to songwriting, and it never ceases to amaze me that captains of industry, people who are very, very smart and have been successful in other pursuits, somehow believe songwriting has different ingredients. Whatever makes you successful in anything, will make you successful as a songwriter, as long as you have that gift. And I do believe songwriting is a gift. I think people are given that gift in different measures. But if you don't have that special gift where you can tune into songs that are out there in the universe. So, here's the secret. The secret is this. You've got to have the gift, you've got to want to do it, you've got to have the desire which, I think passion goes along with that. You've got to work hard. This is the music business, so you have to know your business, and I find the more successful songwriters over the long term know the American songbook over decades, and they know generations of songs. I can tell a couple of people I personally saw in the early stages of their careers and go to great success are both Shania Twain and Taylor Swift. They knew the American songbook. If you're going to be a writer, you've got to know what songs were out there and what people did because that's part of your toolkit. So, if you're adding all this up, it's the same ingredients that make you successful in any other walk of life. Given a gift, you've got to have passions, you've got to work hard, you've got to know your business, and you've got to show up every day. Songwriting is a volume exercise. The greatest songwriter who penned a song in any language wrote thousands of songs to get a handful that we remember.

How much does faith and belief in one's abilities help in becoming a hit songwriter?

What part of that is a formula for songwriting success? I don't know. I'm not so sure that's a big part of the formula as much as picking yourself up when you fall. On the best day, this is a roller-coaster profession. The greatest songwriter that ever lived, the greatest artist has peaks and valleys. We recently did a movie, and I'm going to quote a songwriter, Jimmy Robbins who has a quote in that movie and it says, "this knocks you down 50 times and keeping getting up, and the time you could do is the time that works for you." So certainly, you've got to believe in your abilities. You've got to have a level of craft and ability. You know, there's a part of it where you get up every day and wonder, "am I good enough? Am I going to have this hit?" Every songwriter who has been successful has told me, "I wonder when they're going to catch onto me." So, belief in yourself, self-confidence, I think you've got to have it, but it waxes and wanes. But I'll repeat and say again, the most important thing is that when it wanes, you've got to find it and get up the next morning and say, "I am resilient, I've had my blank kicked, but I don't care, I'm going to write another song...that's what is important."

How much of focus to detail and perfection helps make a hit songwriter?

Words matter in songwriting...." She's Buying a Stairway to Camden." I'm not sure it's the same thing. Or "She's Buying a Stairway to Nirvana." Words matter, a note matters, a pause matters in a song. And songwriters come into to see me all the time. What they don't get is the song is good, it may be really good. But I've heard it a million times, and I've heard it written that way a million times. So little details, attention to what makes a song special and different are essential, especially if you're going to have a long-term career of this.

What role does commitment to short and long-term goals affect success as a hit songwriter?

Well, I think the goal is the same every day--to get up and do something that's going to make somebody feel something. Do professional songwriters have goals? Of course. And the goal is some sort of balance of saying something that matters to them and to the people who hear it versus doing this professionally and making an income from it. Your commitment is when it knocks you down, to be able to get up and do it again. I'm committed to the process and I understand, or I have learned there are a few peaks and a lot of valleys. So, the commitment to resiliency is what's really important.

Do you believe that learning from failures and rejections help in becoming a hit songwriter? Please elaborate.

Well, I don't know that I would say it is learning from rejections and failures, I would say it's learning that's a part of the process. You know, Nolan Ryan, through seven no-hitters, if I remember my statistics correctly, those are the games we remember. But he probably pitched in thousands of them. So, the goal is to get up and have a level of professional consistency...to be able to dig in when you feel bad, and you've had something happen that's in your personal life that puts you in a bad mood...to be able to find a very special, emotional place, to say something the world wants to hear. So, I think what you have to learn is that it is a part of the process. I don't know that if someone didn't cut your song, you're going to learn how to write a better song. It's learning that failures, and really at an astonishing rate: for every 100 songs you write, one gets put on hold. For every 10 holds, one gets cut from every cut. You know, you're writing a few thousand songs to get that song everybody remembers. So, it's understanding that process. I think it's how you handle those first few rejections, cause a lot of people can't. And if you find it in you to get up and be resilient and persistent, then you will eventually succeed if you've got something to say. In a movie we did, Bob DiPiero, a great songwriter says, "I've trying to find something to say that means something to somebody else."

Do you feel like being obsessive and persistent with writing help in becoming a successful hit songwriter? If so, how?

Songwriters have a beautiful dysfunction. Great, true songwriters, it's a gift. I will often counsel families and spouses, "Oh my God they said they had to get up and write that thing at two-thirty in the morning." When a creative flow that is larger than you comes upon you, learn you have to honor that, and you have to be a little bit subservient to that. So, if that is an obsession, it's a beautiful obsession. It's a creative sort of dysfunction. And I find this, Thornton, I find that songwriters are different than just about any other creative profession. Even a songwriter who is the artist; when you're up singing the song you wrote, it's a different part of your brain. It's a different cap you're wearing. I hold songwriters akin to great painters. It's almost an obsessive, dysfunctional, beautiful, wonderful gift all wrapped up into the same juxtaposed things that come together.

Do you think taking risks in your career has helped you become successful? If so, how?

I will say this...people find the word 'commercial' bad when you talk about commercial music. I think every generation could argue that the generation before had better songs and better music. I think the key is to find something commercial with integrity. "Hey Jude" was a commercial song. "American Pie" was a commercial song. I find the songwriters who will occasionally take a risk; those tend to be some of your biggest songs. When you write anything from, "She Thinks My Tractor's Sexy" to "The House That Built Me"; most people would not write it that way. They would sort of turn that whole idea around. I find that when you do take a risk, and it is commercially viable, those tend to be some of the biggest songs of all time.

Do you believe having a positive mental attitude, being optimistic, and possessing strong self-esteem play a major role in success? If so, how?

Songwriters have this weird duality of a complete lack of self-esteem, none whatsoever, while they are some of the most confident people that ever lived. I think you have to experience that entire realm of emotion sometimes in one writing session. I think you go through the entire thing to come up with three minutes that matter, that matter to the world. Again, I would paraphrase what the intent of that question would is: do you have to have resiliency, you have to have the wherewithal, you have to have fortitude and sticktoitness, but when you ask the specific question about self-esteem, I think songwriters are the complete range of total confidence and no confidence whatsoever. And you feel that whole range of emotions. You have to feel it to give us a song that makes us feel something.

Does being a doer and not a talker help in becoming successful? If so, how?

Well, this is a tough industry; it is the music business. And that is a contradiction in terms. You have to be a doer. You have to get up and write every day. It is a volume exercise. Let me tell you what you have to do. So, here's what songwriters do. You start in your hometown, and you're the weirdo. You're the people they make fun of—that's that songwriter guy, that's that girl who writes songs. Sometimes, that might be cool, but more often than not you're that weirdo who sits over there with the pencil humming while everyone else is wondering how they're going to get to the football game. You finally tell your family, "I'm going to Nashville" or "I'm going to Los Angeles" or wherever it is you're going to go and "I'm going to write songs for a living." After an intervention by your family, or after they completely disown you, you come to a town like Nashville, where we sit. You think you're better than you are. You think you know a whole lot more than you actually know and you get your "blank" handed to you because you sit somewhere like the Bluebird Café or you sit in any writer's club, and you see greatness. You'll hear somebody like Tony Arata play "The Dance." You'll hear Lance, Josh, Forest, and Kelsea play, "Love Me Like You Mean It." You'll go, "oh my God." So, you have to figure out how to endure. You have to be a doer in the sense that you have to figure out you've got to get a day job. You've got to park cars or wait tables to support your songwriting habit. You go through this entire, very-difficult, paper-cut-you-to death industry where you start seeing people who came after you that maybe aren't as good as you have some success. So, you have to do. You have to keep writing songs. You have to meet new people. You have to meet the new artists and writers. And finally, finally, finally, one day your song gets recorded, and then they don't put it on the record. And you go through more and more of that. And finally, one day you actually hear your song on the radio, and you start to have some success because this is an industry where success breeds success. And then all of a sudden, you know, the Eagles wrote, "The New Kid in Town," about what happens next. Next in success is all the new kids in town and the great ones have to start that all over again. They have to meet the other new people. They have to do by getting out and meeting the next generation, the next wave of people who are going to write and sing the songs. You have to be a doer. You have to get up every day and do the things that allow you to hopefully, eventually find one of your songs make it through the impossible odds so the world will know about it. You have to be a doer.

Does being a visionary or a dreamer help artists become successful? If so, how?

Well, that kind of goes along with the story I just told you. Dream that you can do this. The odds are infinitesimal; we get asked this a lot. I don't have any statistical analysis to show, some study the city of Nashville did. But right now, my best projection there's probably 80,000 people in Nashville that will tell you they are here to become a successful songwriter, or artist, or engineer or in some creative aspect of music. Truth be known, maybe 8,000 of those would have any modicum of talent that would ever result in that dream coming truth. Truth be known, maybe 800 have the wherewithal and the resilience to go through the trials and errors and the years it takes to make it. And probably only 80 ever make it to the extent of knowing anything they did. Those are hefty odds. And those were the people who moved here to do it. Those are the people who were probably the stars in their hometown. So, you have to be a dreamer. You have to believe you can do this. That's where it starts. If it all begins with the song, it all begins with the songwriter who has a dream. Visionary, I would not speak to that word as much as I would dreamer because this is a dream—you have to defy all the odds.

Do you think overall personality contributes to the success of a songwriter? If so, how?

I certainly think personality contributes and you will find that a lot of co-writers that gravitate toward each other have different kinds of personalities. One is more of the thoughtful contributor; one may have a more exuberant personality. But at the end of the day, songs are you. Songs are the things we all go through, through an individual's lens. When you look at the names that wrote the songs, one of two things happen, they either personally experienced what they are writing about in their songs, or they have experienced enough of life and have gotten good enough at their craft to know how to draw on something, if not that precise thing they have experienced, to write in a way we're going to feel it through an emotional lens. So, it is absolutely a part of it.

Do you feel patience and practice play a role in the creation of a hit songwriter?

I would say practice is essential. You know, I thin*k it was Bobby Braddock that said, I certainly have heard a lot of great songwriters say, "how many songs have you written?" And then I've asked some the songwriters who have come to town, whatever their answer is, that you claim. I don't care what you wrote about your puppy when you were in high school. A record-label executive or a music publisher who comes in here today, and they're looking for a reason to tell you no—not say yes. "How many songs have you written?" And then usually their answer is "I might have eight or 13." I say, "write a hundred you can put your name on and then come talk to me." This is something that you learn through the experience of doing it. There's no way to substitute that. There're things you can learn. There're things you can experience. But a word here, taking a melodic lift down instead of up here is something you learn from doing it, bookending a lyric. Patience? I think that's a requirement. I don't think it's as important as the persistence or the practice. You know, you hear some songs like, a good example is, "The House That Built Me"* *that you work at over a long period of time. But typically, when you are a great craftsman, this is about a moment of inspiration. You may write 50 songs or 100 songs that year and you kind of know when three or four of them are special because you have been visited. Because the idea is the most important currency in songs. And I find, talking to songwriters, that those happen mighty quickly. What I'm saying is you might have written the song in three hours, but it might have taken you 30 years to learn how to do it.*

How much prioritizing your life from day-to-day helps you become successful? If so, how?

One of the things I tell new songwriters when they come to Nashville...." I want to meet a publisher; I want to do this. I want to write with so and so." The first thing I ask them is, "have you got your life in order?" And they'll look all bewildered. And I'll ask, "do you have a job? How are you going to pay for this? Do you have a car? Do you have a place to live?" If you are spiritual, "do you have a place where you worship? Do you have your life in order?" Cause the single, biggest killer in this business, especially with new writers, is that they don't have their life in order. This is a long-haul exercise. It takes years to break into it, and it takes decades to sustain it. So, I believe it is super important to prioritize your life in order to practice your career.

Do you continue to learn all you can about your profession? If so, how?

For me, I'm an advocate for songwriters, and every two years there's a new Congress. We so we just started one. There's a new party in control in the House of Representatives, which means there's a new chairman as we do this interview. There's a new political dynamic every two years. So, I will tell you this, as hard as it is to get to the top or to get success in a career, when they say it's harder to stay on top, that's completely accurate. And I'm not sure that means necessarily the same expenditure of time. But emotions, stress, focus, resiliency, it's harder to maintain that, than it was to get there in the first place.

In any part of your life, has self-discipline played a major role in helping become successful? If so, how?

The single biggest career killer besides not having your life in order, let's suppose you become a professional, is not showing up. You don't show up for two appointments, and this is a community, and everybody knows it, and no one starts booking writes with you. This is as much a people business as it is a craft. It is certainly both. And if you're not pleasant to be in the room with if you are a little dictatorial; you know co-writing is rarely "co," the best co-writers and most songs co-written among professionals because it becomes a profession, you know, there's a reason people co-write. That is because when you got to write 100 to 200 songs a year, you don't always come with the best emotion or idea, and it's a heck of a lot easier to feed off each other than to sit there in the mirror and twiddle your thumbs. So, if you're going to be a co-writer in the modern music industry, you've got to be someone people who want to be in the room with. You've got to know when to drive, or when to navigate.

Is there any factor, trait, or ingredient we may have omitted that helps in becoming a successful, hit songwriter?

You know, one of the things I preach about right now is ability; especially if you're going to be a songwriter or an artist and you come in here, and you're not a very good guitar player. Can you do it? Sure. But why aren't you learning to be a really a very good guitar player and learn to play the piano as well? Before you came here today, a young lady showed up here in the lobby. She said, "what can I do?" I said, "learn the history of American popular music. You get your digital service and call up next week the top pop hits of 1956, then the next week 1957, and you built you a playlist. Do the same thing with country. You've got to know the American songbook if you want to be a professional. And the ones that have greater tools to draw on, typically have greater success. And so, I don't see that type of work ethic today, generally speaking as I used to. I don't if it's the digitalization of music. I don't know if you depend on the track person and you don't necessarily write the melody yourself. I have seen in the last decade, careers shorter, success briefer. So, pack your tool kit if you want to be successful in the long haul.

Do you believe a hit songwriter is born or made? Explain your thoughts.

I think it's both. I think you have to have a gift. Many songwriters will tell you, that many of their best songs, they don't know where they came from. You will hear stories. "I started singing this thing," or" this chunk of this song just appeared in my head," or it was a dream, or I woke up with it." I think we all have gifts. Some of us are wired differently. And songwriters just have this ability to channel something that's out there in the cosmos. And that's well and good, but if you're really going to be successful, and successful over the long term you've had to hone that into a craft. A word matters. One of the things I see with a lot of young songwriters, and I've seen this for a few decades, is that they will come in with that chunk that's awesome and they'll play me a song. And I'll go, "that's what you heard in the middle of the night." And they'll say, "how did you know that?" And I'll say, "because the rest of it isn't as good." "Your transitions are terrible—getting from that to over here, it's just not the same level, same quality." And that's work. That's writing your first thousand songs. That takes listening to other songs and looking at rhyme schemes, and song structures, to learn how to take that where it's supposed to go. And you're just got to do it over and over; you've got to put a lot of work into it, to be able to combine those two. It is a gift that you hone. The same thing is true with athletics. You might have the most promising, ninth -grade football player you've ever seen. But if they don't practice and don't hone it, that gift doesn't mean as much by the time you're college age. And I think that's true with any profession and it's true in this one.

Do you believe talent is a gift or is it earned? Explain your thoughts.

I do think it is a gift. I have seen different writers at different levels of that gift. And about once every five years, somebody will come in here at a very young age. And in our industry, the bigger the insult, the better the compliment—they're just a freak. Where did you come from? How do you know how to do this at such an early age? You can point to Taylor Swift or Jimmy Robbins or others. So, you get different levels of talent, but none of them sustain it over the long haul unless they work at it; the more they work at it, the better the results are.

Do you believe that talent comes from within? If so, is it how they process stimuli in life?

Well, I said earlier, I think as a songwriter, your brain's wired differently. You've got a lot of juxtaposed emotions and characteristics, both good and bad, all in the same package. So, it's just a combination of all of that.

What is talent?

Well, when it comes to music, the only test for me is how does it make me feel. How do I respond to it in the entire range of emotions? And I don't care if you're the artist, musician or especially the songwriter, the ones I gravitate to the most are the ones that make me feel the most, consistently make me feel something in the human range of emotions; that's the test for me.

Do you believe self-criticism helps or harms the success of a hit songwriter?

I would change self-criticism to editing. Every songwriter's favorite song is the last one they wrote, but the experienced songwriters, true professional songwriters learn to get over that—the five-minute love affair and know what's good and what's not and to know when to keep working on a song. I find with new songwriters, the single biggest thing they lack, is the inability to know that and their ability to edit their songs. And I think for most songwriters, no matter what your gift is, that just comes with time. I think the longer you do it, the greater your ability to know the difference between good, bad and mediocre and to know whether you can turn mediocre into good and occasionally into great, and along with that comes editing skills. You just have to do it over and over again.

Do you believe hit songwriters are more attuned to what is going on and happening around them than others?

Let me use our last songwriter of the decade—the ASCAP Songwriter of the Century which was Craig Wiseman. Craig has an ability to take something emotional, meaningful and get it on the radio. And I said earlier, but I'll say it again, some people think the word, 'commercial' is bad. They think that means trite or you're sold out your real gift of songwriting. I think the biggest gift of all for commercial music is to know how to do commercial with integrity. So, I find today, that people like Craig Wiseman, Nicolle Galyon, Hilary Lindsay, Brett James, Lee Thomas Miller; they've got this very unique way to take something and make me feel something, but also tell it in three minutes where the radio's going to play it. And that is part of being of professional songwriter—that's how you get paid. Even in the streaming era, most of the songwriter's compensation still comes from broadcast radio. So, the ones who figure out how to that, it's a true art form.

Do you believe inspiration is a state of mind and could it be a major factor in the creation of a hit songwriter? Why?

Inspiration to me is emotional. When you're inspired you feel something. I think that can come through stimuli. It can come spiritually; it can come a lot of different ways. I do believe that the more experienced songwriters become, they can find inspiration or channel previous feelings or emotions into something that's inspirational. So, it is both an organic experience for human beings, but for songwriters, they seem to be able to summon that more frequently than others.

Do you believe having empathy helps in becoming a hit songwriter? Explain.

Certainly, empathy helps you to be a better songwriter. But I would expand that; I would just say it's the whole range of human emotions, whether it's silly. Some of my favorite songs are just silly; they're stupid. And that's how I want to feel. I want to tune out and tune on the radio and not worry about all the stress of the day. Some are just so. Poignant. The Steve Seskin, Tom Douglas song, "Grown Men Don't Cry' has some personal application to me. Every time I hear it, those emotions come back. So, whatever the panoply of the emotions is, whether it's empathy, envy, jealousy, love, lust, or humor. The great songwriters know how to take that and parlay that into a three-minute jewel that the world gets to hear, and they get to commerce.

Chapter Twenty-Two:

Interview with Songwriter **Burt Bacharach**

Legendary hit songwriter, composer, and pianist, **Burt Bacharach**

Artist Biography by John Bush

With a hit-single track record spanning four decades, Burt Bacharach became one of the most important composers of popular music in the 20th century, almost equal to such classic tunesmiths as George Gershwin or Irving Berlin. His sophisticated yet breezy productions borrowed from cool jazz, soul, Brazilian bossa nova, and traditional pop to virtually define and undoubtedly transcend the staid forms of Brill Building adult pop during the 1960s.

Born May 12, 1928, in Kansas City, he studied cello, drums, and piano as a child, and was later transplanted to New York City by his father, a syndicated columnist. The time spent in New York gave him a chance to sneak into clubs to watch his bebop heroes: Dizzy Gillespie and Charlie Parker; he also played in several jazz bands during the 1940s. Bacharach studied music theory and composition at the Mannes School in New York, at Berkshire Music Center, at the New School for Social Research (with Darius Milhaud), at Montreal's McGill University, and at the Music Academy of the West in Santa Barbara, CA. A period in the Army interrupted his concentration of music study, but even while serving in Germany, Bacharach arranged and played piano for a dance band. He also played in nightclubs and backed Steve Lawrence, the Ames Brothers, and Paula Stewart. Bacharach was discharged in 1952, and he married Stewart on December 22nd of the following year.

On returning to the U.S., he began writing songs for Lawrence, Patti Page, the Ames Brothers, and others, but his first hit came from Marty Robbins in late 1957 when Robbins took "The Story of My Life" to the American Top 20 and the number one spot in England. The single was also notable for its co-composer, Hal David, who became Bacharach's songwriting partner and collaborated on most of his big hits. The Bacharach/David team followed up in January 1958 with Perry Como's "Magic Moments," another U.K. chart-topper and a Top Five entry in America. Bacharach's marriage dissolved in 1958, and he left for Europe to tour with Marlene Dietrich. He returned in 1961, and wrote several songs for the Drifters with Bob Hilliard (including "Mexican Divorce" and "Please Stay") before reuniting with Hal David. At an arranging session, he found the singer who became the ultimate vehicle for his songs: Dionne Warwick who was working as a member of the Drifters' backup vocal group, the Gospelaires.

By late 1962, Bacharach and David began focusing most of their composing energy on Warwick, who was the recipient of 15 Top 40 singles from 1962 to 1968 (including the Top Tens "Anyone Who Had a Heart," "Walk on By,"

Interview with Songwriter **Burt Bacharach**

"Message to Michael," "I Say a Little Prayer," "Valley of the Dolls," and "Do You Know the Way to San Jose?"). The duo also remained dominant in England, where Frankie Vaughan, Cilla Black, Sandie Shaw, the Walker Brothers, and Herb Alpert all hit number one with Bacharach/David compositions. As if their schedule wasn't busy enough throughout the '60s, the songwriters contributed film scores for What's New Pussycat?, Alfie, and Casino Royale. The film featuring their most celebrated score, Butch Cassidy and the Sundance Kid (1969), won Oscars for Best Original Score and Best Theme Song for "Raindrops Keep Fallin' on My Head" (plus two non-musical Academy Awards). Bacharach and David began working on the musical Promises, Promises in the late '60s; it won a Tony and a Grammy Award (for cast album) during a popular three-year Broadway run. Bacharach hit the charts himself in 1969, with the show's "I'll Never Fall in Love Again" reaching the Top 100. Surprisingly, this was not his only foray into recording; Bacharach had reached number four in the U.K. charts in May 1965 with "Trains and Boats and Planes," and he released several popular solo albums during the late '60s.

The beginning of the '70s looked bright for Burt Bacharach, as the Carpenters took "(They Long to Be) Close to You" to number one in the U.S. in July 1970. The forecast was premature, though, as three of his closest partners -- Hal David, Dionne Warwick, and his second wife Angie Dickinson -- left him. He gathered several accolades for an eponymous 1971 album featuring renditions of his previous hit compositions, but later albums were disappointing and Bacharach's next hit was over a decade in coming. Finally in 1981, he collaborated with Christopher Cross, Carole Bayer Sager, and Peter Allen on the Oscar-winning "Arthur's Theme." Bacharach married Bayer Sager just one year later, and together they wrote Roberta Flack's Top 20 hit "Making Love," as well as "Heartlight" which Neil Diamond took to number five.

Once Bacharach resumed composing he began to hit, and 1986 was one of his finest years, with two American number ones: "That's What Friends Are For" (by an all-star group including Warwick, Elton John, Gladys Knight, and Stevie Wonder) and a duet by Patti LaBelle and Michael McDonald titled "On My Own." He divorced Sager in 1991, but worked with Dionne Warwick again two years later on "Sunny Weather Love," from her Friends Can Be Lovers album. Also in 1993, Bacharach contributed songs to James Ingram, Earth, Wind & Fire, and Tevin Campbell. Around the same time, many alternative bands began name-checking the hitmaker as an influence, and Oasis frontman Noel Gallagher joined him on the stage of the Royal Albert Hall as well as including a picture of him on the cover of Oasis' "Definitely Maybe." BBC-TV focused on Bacharach in a January 1996 documentary, and a three-disc retrospective of his compositions was released by Rhino in 1998. That same year he collaborated with Elvis Costello on the acclaimed Painted From Memory, and was celebrated at an all-star concert at Radio City Music Hall which later formed the basis for the LP One Amazing Night. The 2005 album At This Time found Bacharach writing lyrics for the first time. Tonio K helped with the lyrics, Elvis Costello, Dr. Dre, Chris Botti, and Rufus Wainwright also contributed to the album.

Do you believe drive, passion, and stamina (energy level) play a major role in helping a person to become a successful hit songwriter?

Certainly, passion helps. It is very essential. Drive is good. You work hard, you can't conceive to writing a song in one day and letting it go, without looking at it the next day, and maybe the day after that, and the day after that.

Interview with Songwriter **Burt Bacharach**

Do you think work ethic plays a vital part in becoming a hit songwriter? If so, how?

Well, yes, it is essential. Again, no matter how hard you work, how hard your work ethic is, you still must have, inside you, some degree of talent and ability. I'm a believer in work ethic, if it's me, getting to the keyboard every day, if I can do that, just to play. If I come up with something great, if I don't come up with something, it's a process. You do not win every day.

How much does faith and belief in one's abilities help in becoming a hit songwriter?

Well, you do build faith in yourself when you get a degree of acceptance; when you find a song you really liked got recorded by such and such an artist; you find acceptance for yourself when the song goes on and becomes a top-10 hit. You know, to not get encouragement, I've seen a lot of that in the Brill Building days where songwriters thought they had talent or some degree of talent and ran short on money and then to deal with the publisher. It was a different world back then, anyway. I think it's important, like going to the office. We go to the office three days a week, almost every day, give yourself six days. Go to your instrument, sit. You get nothing. Don't get discouraged. I've gone three days and I've gotten nothing. Chalk it up to a good day even if you get nothing. You don't get to that point unless you stick with it. Don't get discouraged. It's a hard game. It has always been hard.

How much of focus to detail and perfection helps make a hit songwriter?

I think some of the details towards making a song good, or were acceptable for me, were getting away from my instrument, the keyboard, sitting on the couch, sitting in a chair, hearing it in my head instead of hearing it at the piano, or the synthesizer or whatever it be. Because when you're sitting at the keyboard you are getting it bar-by-bar, you don't hear the longevity of that song from the start to finish. I think that is the very key. I think it is important for young songwriters to be able to--instead of dumping their ideas on a phone, I am much in favor that they do that, but they also are able to, if they are on a plane and have a cocktail napkin, to write out not just the lyric, but the actual melody because they hear it in their heads.

What role does commitment to short and long-term goals affect success as a hit songwriter?

Throw out the short-term thing because you can go a year without getting a song to an artist you want to get it to. You could wait on an artist for four years, and then he might change his mind or her mind and record the song. It requires patience. It's not an overnight thing. You can write a song and have the artist like it and have the record company not like it.

Do you believe that learning from failures and rejections help in becoming a hit songwriter? Please elaborate.

You know, I've written some songs that I thought were really good—worthy of being heard, worthy of being possible hits. You're not the decider there. You may think they are worthy, and they think they're not worthy. Works the other way too—someone else says, "No, I really believe in the song." Don't forget, when you're writing the song, and you're really spending some time with the song, it's a short form, not a long form, three minutes of telling a story with a good melody; and if you write like the way I write, which is hearing it hundreds of times in different forms, sitting on a couch, not at the keyboard, looking at the long scope of where that song is going, you can't make those decisions as a writer—yes, this is it, this is going to be a great hit. You can't make that call. You hope it will be. You have to be the arbiter, the person that makes the judgment call unless you're co-writing with someone. And that's very helpful, sometimes, to have two people looking at something that you're both working on at the same time.

Do you feel like being obsessive and persistent with writing help in becoming a successful hit songwriter? If so, how?

It's easier for me because I can take a long time to write stuff; I am very obsessive about it: would it be better this way or would it be better that way, compulsive about it... a lot of composers go into a song they want to become a hit. But the moment of truth for me is where it goes once when it leaves my hands and goes into a studio with an arranger writing an arrangement, an A & R man with a vocal with the musicians playing, what the orchestration sounds like, what the tempo feels like. There are a lot of things, unless you're the producer yourself, you don't have control of. I think I had a certain amount of songs early on in my career that maybe got ruined in somebody's else's hands —the arranger, the A & R man, the choice of artist to sing the song, the tempo of it. You have to acknowledge that it is a set operation for me. The other thing is that for me, early on, I had permission from an A & R man in Chicago to go into the studio with one of his artists, which I had not done before, and record the song. Where the A & R guy would say, "You know, I want you to do this song; I want you to write the arrangement, you pick the musicians, you pick the studio, you conduct the orchestra, you set the tempo, you make the "record." Now once that happened to me, it gets much better because now, you got permission to follow it through, you, know if it doesn't work you don't blame the arranger, you don't blame the A & R. You blame yourself, or you take credit for it, "oh, that's really good", or you learn from your mistakes by taking charge of the whole thing of being where you screwed up. We're not talking about rocket science here. We're talking about a short form of music—three minutes. You don't want any dead spots in that three minutes.

Do you think taking risks in your career has helped you become successful? If so, how?

If you play it too safe, you will not be successful.

Do you believe having a positive mental attitude, being optimistic, and possessing strong self-esteem play a major role in success? If so, how?

Success brings success. When you have a hit, your self-esteem goes up. You go a year without getting anything recorded or anything published, and it affects self-esteem, sure.

Does being a doer and not a talker help in becoming successful? If so, how?

You've got to put the time in. You've got to make it like you're going into the office. Basically, the best rule, though I don't do it every day, I should do it every day; the goal is to go to the office every day. And maybe come up with nothing—that's okay. Maybe you have a lyric you've been working on; you try it again. Spend the time, look at it another way, get away from the keyboard, sit in a chair, listen to it in your head. You see it helps for me that I can go into the studio, and know how the rhythm section will be playing, and know how to translate that song in my head and in my heart-where the strings come in, or where the strings don't come in, or if they're strings at all, where someone's singing out of tune, where there should be harmony...I mean, these are things that you live and the record lives or dies by your decisions.

Does being a visionary or a dreamer help artists become successful? If so, how?

I don't think you can say you're going to be visionary—it either will happen or it won't. You just do the best you can and writing the best you are able to write. Put the visionary in the drawer. Let someone else make that decision or whether you're a visionary.

Interview with Songwriter **Burt Bacharach**

Do you think overall personality contributes to the success of a songwriter? If so, how?

I think personality enters into the picture when it is a collaborative effort-two writers working on a song instead of just one writer. If two writers happen to get along, who's not budging, and who's not threatened, who feels overwhelmed or who is doing the overwhelming themselves. It's not fair. It's better if you leave your ego at the door. If you write with someone you've never written with before and you think you won't get anything, you won't get anything or will get something. Better to begin with an open mind and at best, certainly get along.

Do you feel patience and practice play a role in the creation of a hit songwriter?

Totally...you have to have patience; you can't give up on something. If you go three days and you still haven't gotten the bridge of a song, then you look at it another way. You try it another way you go about that bridge. You don't just throw the song away just because you don't have the right bridge.

How much prioritizing your life from day-to-day helps you become successful?

I don't think I had any talent when I started. I have talent now, so that's come. You just see how things evolve. You have success; then you have more success. But you're still not very totally sure, if you've got it all; if you're terrific, or rare and good, or pretty good.; you don't take anything for granted.

Do you continue to learn all you can about your profession? If so, how?

You learn about life; you stay open. You don't stay closed. It's all about living—doing what you see and what you feel. Basically, if you're open, you write who you are. If you've got talent, all the better. And if you're not -so-talented, you still write who you are. If it's a true, honest picture of how you're feeling, and how you're approaching it. That, to me, gives you the power.

In any part of your life, has self-discipline played a major role in helping become successful? If so, how?

Yes, I don't take writing lightly. I don't throw it away, I mean if a song doesn't work out. It took me three weeks to write the melody of Alfie to Hal's lyrics. It's a kind of discipline and obsessiveness. You know, I'm pretty good at that stuff—being obsessive about it—some things and tempos.

Is there any factor, trait, or ingredient we may have omitted that helps in becoming a successful, hit songwriter?

It's some of the things I talked about before. Like my son; when he goes on the road with me, he plays the keyboard, he's 26 now, he started, maybe doing this when he was 19. He plays maybe six or seven songs with my band. But what I did when he was bringing things up on the computer; I'd maybe show him a chord a day. But when I showed him a chord a day, I wanted him to see what that chord looked like on music paper, and he could see from the music paper, and to know which finger goes where on the keyboard. Some people would find that was boring: "I can just type it into my phone"; but that's not good enough for me. You really have to be well-rounded. Learn how to write music down on a piece of paper.

Do you believe a hit songwriter is born or made? Explain your thoughts.

It is made and being lucky.

Do you believe talent is a gift or is it earned? Explain your thoughts.

Talent has a way of growing. The more time you

spend with your muse, the more time you spend with your activity, the more you are involved with it—the talent you are involved in. So your talent should grow. You should live with it. You'll get bored if you're doing the same thing. Do different things. It is a learning process, a growing process. Nobody wouldn't have given me five cents to be able to say, when I was first starting out, that I had any talent—I thought I had none.

Do you believe that talent comes from within? If so, is it how they process stimuli in life?

I think I've already answered that. You write who you are.

What is talent?

Good achievements, good results. There are people who are so talented who are playing in bars in a Holiday Inn somewhere. You've got to be lucky, too.

Do you believe self-criticism helps or harms the success of a hit songwriter?

Yeah, I think it helps. Okay, now let me hear it again—what's wrong with it, what can I change? You have to be able to try to be the listener.

Do you believe hit songwriters are more attuned to what is going on and happening around them than others?

Oh yes, it helps. Being well-educated in writing music is good, too.

Do you believe inspiration is a state of mind, and could it be a major factor in the creation of a hit songwriter?

Yes, it makes it a whole lot easier in the process of writing.

Do you believe having empathy helps in becoming a hit songwriter?

Empathy is an essential item to have in whatever you're doing in life—if you're an accountant, or whether you're working in McDonald's. It's essential to have empathy whether you're a songwriter or not.

Chapter Twenty-Three:

The Lives of Legendary Hit Songwriters

When we delve into the lives of legendary songwriters, we learn some interesting facts about their childhood days. Many of them gravitated toward singing or learning a musical instrument at early ages. While it isn't a prerequisite to have been born with parents who were musical, it does help. Also note these legends worked extremely hard to develop their gifts and talents.

As stated by *Encyclopedia Britannica*, John Legend was born John Roger Stephens on December 28, 1978. He was considered a prodigy, which means he could have been born with his gift when you consider he started playing piano at a very early age. Or he could have had been born under a musical family. John Legend's grandmother gave him piano lessons and he had a strong musical influence as he grew up singing in his church choir. Legend lead an a cappella group at the University of Pennsylvania where he attended. At first, his career was not in music. Legend decided to work for Boston Consulting Group and perform in nightclubs in New York City on the side. At age 26, John Legend's debut album, "Get Lifted" went platinum, mainly due to his hit single, "Ordinary People." The rest is history as they say. Legend went on to make a name for himself winning multiple Grammy Awards, releasing multiple hit songs and performing at the Super Bowl XL in Detroit. *Biography.com* quotes John Legend about his career as saying: "I come from a city where 40 percent to 50 percent of our kids drop out of high school. I did well in high school and then went to an Ivy League school, but I was the exception. We need to do more to make sure every kid has a quality education."

Legendary, hall of fame songwriter, Jimmy Webb, learned to play piano and organ at a very early age. Both of Webb's parents played music. As documented by *All Music*, Webb's mother was his biggest encourager. At age 12, Jimmy was being accompanied by his mom on accordion and his dad on guitar as young Jimmy frequently played piano and organ in all of the rural churches his dad presided over as a Baptist minister in southwestern Oklahoma and west Texas. Jimmy's early musical influences were restricted to country music and white gospel music as his dad wouldn't allow Jimmy to listen to anything else. When Jimmy hit his early teen years, he was becoming creative with the music he was playing at his father's churches. Jimmy would frequently improvise and rearrange the hymns. He started writing religious tunes. That was short lived when Jimmy discovered the music of Elvis Presley and Glen Campbell.

When Jimmy turned 18-years-old, he and his family moved to Southern California. Webb studied music at San Bernardino Valley College. 1964, Webb and his family moved to Southern California, where he attended San Bernardino Valley College studying music. After his mother died in 1965, Webb decided to stay in California while his dad returned to Oklahoma. After the death of his mother in 1965, his father made plans to return to Oklahoma. Jimmy continued to work at his musical studies and songwriting in Los Angeles. Not long after that, Webb signed a songwriting contract with Jobete Music, a division of Motown Records. Webb met the Supremes, Johnny Rivers, The Fifth Dimension and finally Glen Campbell. Webb's career was launched in a big way. He went on to win multiple Grammy awards, garnering hit-after-hit on the radio and being honored in the Songwriters Hall of Fame. In 1968, Time acknowledged Webb's range, proficiency, and "gift for strong, varied rhythms, inventive structures, and rich, sometimes surprising harmonies."

In early 2000, Jimmy Webb returned to his Christian faith. As stated by the Salvation Army's newspaper, "The War Cry," Webb said, "I am a strong believer in God... God is important to me. God is bigger than any one particular denomination. I don't like it when people try to confine Him. I don't put any limits on God."

Webb has never forgotten his father's warning to him about his musical aspirations early in his career, saying, "This songwriting thing is going to break your heart." But, however, Webb's father saw how determined his son was to make it in the songwriting business, so he gave him $40 saying, "It's not much, but it's all I have."

Legendary Dolly Rebecca Parton was born into poverty as the fourth child of 12 in a one-room cabin in Pittman Center, Tennessee on January 19, 1946. She describes her family as being "dirt-poor." Dolly admired her hard-working mother and father. Parton gives credit for her success to her father for his business shrewdness and her mother's family for their musical talents. Even though she grew up in poverty, Parton was constantly surrounded by music. When Dolly was a young child, her parents moved to a farm at Locust Ridge. She is most fond of her childhood days spent in that breathtaking scenery. In fact, growing up in Locust Ridge left such an impression on her that she was inspired to write the song, "My Tennessee Mountain Home" in the 1970s.

According to *New World Encyclopedia*, Dolly was raised Pentecostal in the Church Of God in Cleveland, Tennessee, where her grandfather, Jake Robert Owens pastored. Dolly started performing in public in church at the early of six. She performed on a homemade guitar at age seven, and when she turned eight, her uncle bought her a real guitar. She practiced hard and started singing on the local radio and television stations in the East Tennessee area shortly thereafter. When Dolly reached age 10, she performed regularly on The Cas Walker Show on WVIK Radio and on WBIR-TV in Knoxville. Dolly recorded her first single, "Puppy Love" at age 13 on Gold band Records and appeared on the Grand Ole' Opry the same year. She met Johnny Cash, who mentored her by encouraging her to stick with music as a career. The day after she graduated from Sevier County High School, Dolly moved to Nashville. She found immediate success by signing to Combine Publishing and having several charted singles on the radio.

Dolly Parton went on to become a legend as a recording artist, songwriter, actress, producer, and music business entrepreneur. Parton has had over 25 RIAA-certified gold, platinum, and multi-platinum recordings; 25 number one *Billboard* charted singles; 41 top-ten country albums; 110 charted singles; nine Grammy, two Academy of Country Music Awards and three American Music Association Awards; 47 Grammy Award nominations; written over 3,000 songs and received the CMA Entertainer of the Year Award. In 1999, Dolly Parton was inducted into the Country Music Hall of Fame.

Carole Joan Klein, better known as the legendary Carole King was born in Manhattan in February 1942. Carole had an unquenchable curiosity for music which began at the early age of three years old. Since her mother, Eugenia had previously studied piano lessons as a child; Carole would often hear her mother practice piano in their small, two-story duplex in Brooklyn. Carole's mother decided to teach Carole some very basic piano skills at three years old. Carole's parents made a startling discovery that their young, four-year-old daughter had perfect pitch where she could correctly identify a note on the piano by just hearing it. According to *A Natural Woman: A Memoir* by Carole King, only 1 in 10,000 of the population has the gift of perfect pitch. Carole's father, Sidney would often show off his daughter's gift to friends who visited their house. Looking back on that particular childhood memory, Carole King said, "My dad's smile was so broad that it encompassed the lower half of his face. I enjoyed making my father happy and getting the notes right."

Carole's mother gave her real piano lessons at the age of four years. Carole remembers climbing up on the stool and sitting on a phone book to raise her body higher to reach the piano keys. Carole King learned music theory, beginning piano technique, how to read notes, and how to play rhythms correctly in time. Carole had a strong desire to learn as much music as possible.

"My mother never forced me to practice. She didn't have to. I wanted so much to master the popular songs that poured out of the radio," Carole King said.

The music Carole learned at an early reaped big reward. When Carole was only four-years-old, she began kindergarten and only after a year, she was promoted to second grade because she exhibited an exceptional gift with words and numbers.

Carole started a band called the Co-Sines in the 1950's while attending James Madison High School. She changed her name to Carole King and began making demo recordings at $25 a session with her friend, Paul Simon. King's first single release which she wrote was "The Right Girl" on ABC-Paramount Records in 1958.

Carole wrote her breakthrough album, "Tapestry" which ended up becoming number one on the U.S. album chart for 15 weeks in 1971. And for a total of six years, the album remained on the album charts. Carole King has recorded 25 solo albums and has had record sales of over 75 million copies worldwide. King has won four Grammy Awards and has been honored by being inducted into the Hall of Fame and the Rock and Roll Hall of Fame for her songwriting. Carol King is the first woman to have been honored with the Library of Congress Gershwin Prize for Popular Song. King is a 2015 Kennedy Center Honoree.

According to *Britannica.com*, legendary music icon, Lionel Brockman Richie, Jr., better known as Lionel Ritchie was born on June 20, 1949, in Tuskegee, Alabama. During his childhood days, young Ritchie lived on the campus of Tuskegee Institute, now known as Tuskegee University. His grandmother, a classical pianist, introduced Lionel to the piano, the basics of music and to the great classical composers. Ritchie's uncle gave Lionel his first saxophone since his uncle was a big-band jazz musician and arranger. At first, Ritchie was drawn to Gospel music because he wanted to become a priest in the Episcopal Church, but Lionel decided to follow the musical influences of the African American popular styles as well as country music. He also realized he wasn't "priest material." At age 13, Lionel moved with his family to Illinois and attended Joliet East High School. Then Lionel moved back to Alabama to study economics and accounting at Tuskegee Institute after graduating from high school in 1967. Ritchie was an all-star tennis player and received a scholarship to attend Tuskegee. Lionel joined the college band, the Mystics where he played saxophone, composed and sometimes sang as the lead singer. The Mystics went on to become the funk, pop, rhythm-and-blues band, the Commodores. Ritchie became the lead singer of the group.

At first, the Commodores were briefly signed to Atlantic Records and recorded one record, but then they caught the eye of Motown Record Corporation who signed them in 1974 after Lionel Ritchie graduated with a bachelor's degree in economics.

Lionel Ritchie went on to record 20 albums, with 42 radio-hit singles, five number one *Billboard* hit singles, 15 top-ten *Billboard* hit singles, and has sold over 90 million records worldwide. Ritchie has won four Grammy awards, has been nominated for two Golden Globe awards, and was inducted into the Songwriters Hall of Fame in 1994. Lionel Ritchie had the distinct honor of receiving the Kennedy Center Honor in 2017 and has appeared as a judge on the television show, American Idol with Katy Perry and Luke Bryan.

As stated by *All Music*, legendary songwriter and artist, Joni Mitchell was born Roberta Joan Anderson on November 7, 1943. While living in

Saskatchewan, Canada during her childhood days, Mitchell was most interested in painting, but also studied classical piano for a short while. After Joni Mitchell caught polio and was hospitalized at age nine, she started focusing her time on the creative side of her and considered being a singer or a dancer. She took up the habit of smoking at an early age of nine and claims that smoking affected the way her voice sounded when she sang. Then she moved to the city of Saskatoon in Canada. Joni preferred to be an independent, free-thinker and didn't perform well to formal education. One of her teachers, who taught unconventionally, managed to inspire Joni to write poetry. Mitchell went onto dedicate her first album to her teacher. Joni quit school in 12th grade and started hanging out in the downtown area with wild crowds until she realized she was falling too fast into the criminal world. So, Mitchell decided to learn the guitar with a Pete Seeger songbook. Her left hand was too weak to play standard guitar, so Mitchell came up with alternative ways to tune the guitar which later developed into untraditional ways to perform harmony with unconventional ways to structure songs. Joni's first paid concert was on October 31, 1962, at a Saskatoon club that featured jazz and folk artists.

Mitchell was so influenced by jazz that she saved her money and bought the album, The Hottest New Group in Jazz of Lamberth, Hendricks, and Ross at a booklet price.

Mitchell said, "1 considered that album to be my Beatles. I learned every song off of it, and I don't think there is another album anywhere—including—my own which I know every note and word of every song."

Her passion for art still haunted her, so Joni left home to study abstract painting at the Alberta College of Art in Calgary. After a year of her art studies, Joni at age 20 dropped out of school. Joni decided to play gigs as a folk musician in a Calgary coffeehouse on weekends. Then she made her way to local TV and radio shows in Calgary. The same year, Mitchell left for Toronto to become a folk singer. Along the way, she stopped at the Mariposa Folk Festival to see Buffy Sainte-Mairie, a Cree folk singer from Saskatchewan. One year later, Joni Mitchell found herself performing at the same festival and years after that, Sainte-Marie recorded some of Joni Mitchell's songs. Mitchell recorded her first debut album in 1968; and went on to record 21 total albums, with 33 *Billboard* radio charted singles and at least one number one single; and has sold over 10 million albums worldwide. Joni Mitchell has won nine Grammy Awards, and *Rolling Stone* Magazine called her, "one of the greatest songwriters ever." *All Music* said, "When the dust settles, Joni Mitchell may stand as the most important and influential female recording artist of the late 20th century."

We are sure you could name many of your favorite legendary songwriters from the current ones as well as from the past centuries. And you will probably determine from their biographies that many of these legendary songwriters were influenced at an early by someone in their families. Many were exposed to musical instruments or learned to play musical instruments at an early age. Nevertheless, each hit songwriter has a different story. No two hit songwriters lived the exact same lives. No two experienced the same things. We could have written an entire book on the early musical lives and training these songwriters received on their journey to becoming hit songwriters. We feel that the six legendary hit songwriters we wrote about in this chapter are great examples of how many hit songwriters have lived their lives since early childhood. Feel free to explore as many hit songwriter's lives as possible and learn from their lives. You may even discover something about one of them you never knew. And in your research, you may find deep inspiration from them and one of them just might become your mentor for life.

Chapter Twenty-Four:

How Environment Plays a Role

Environment; let's break down that word before beginning to talk about how it can affect our success as a songwriter. If I'm being literal; environment is based on our influences from the time of conception. We've all heard of nature vs. nurture—the debate that is based on a person's genes vs. external factors after birth. Why debate when both come into play with our success? In this chapter, I'm going to break down environment into two sections: physical environment and mental environment. We can have the right skills, talent, and personality but our environment in which we surround ourselves in plays a major role in becoming a hit songwriter.

Physical Environment

I will not be scientific in this portion and write about a true "physical" environment (e.g., soil, climate, water supply.) No, your physical environment includes what and who you surround yourself with.

Think about that for a moment and ask yourself these questions:

- *Do I run around with people who never seem quite on top of the game?*
- *Are my friends positive and supportive?*
- *Do I hang out with others who set goals and complete them?*
- *Do I have a mentor(s) who will help when I'm struggling?*
- *Do I have someone I can confide in when times get tough?*

These may seem like simple, yes or no questions but they are quite important to your success. We've all heard the saying "it takes a village to raise a child," well, it takes an incredible team of people to help you reach your potential as a hit songwriter. Check your answers and see where you can improve.

The people around you can only affect you so much; then it becomes your choice. How you act will also determine your success. Here are some key questions and food for thought.

- *Do you help others achieve their goals and dreams?*
- *Are you a mentor?*
- *Are you a positive force when your friends are down?*
- *Do you support others and cheer for their success?*
- *Do you keep what others have confided in you, to yourself?*

It's not enough to be a taker; you must also give. Giving back and helping others will create a beautiful journey of success. Think about the people who have supported, worked with you, and helped you reach goals. Have a sense of gratefulness and help someone else. I guarantee you the road to success will become a little less bumpy when you do for others. People in any field that are successful are the ones that see potential in others and help them grow. Contrary to belief; the world does not revolve around you and neither should your songs. Hit songs aren't created by only writing about your life; your successes and failures.

Let's delve deeper into the physical environment. Nature vs. nurture is quite interesting. The interviews within this book ask many questions about nature and if hit songwriters are born into the craft or not. There are plenty of differing views on nature; but what about nurture? How does home environment factor in our abilities to become a successful hit songwriter? We could have an entire chapter on songwriters whose parents were musicians, in the entertainment industry, or that had large financial sources. All of these play a role in a person's success; for a while. We could also talk about the hit songwriters that grew up in poverty, abuse, and lack of parental support. What good would a list of already successful songwriters do you? No good at all. Let's focus on you! I'm going to give two, outlandish and exaggerated scenarios. I've placed you in these examples.

Scenario One: Your home-life was fantastic. You have two parents that adore you and did everything for you. Your parents still do everything for you. They support your dreams physically, mentally, emotionally, and financially. You grew up healthy; rarely sick and were given the best music lessons money could afford. Many years have passed since those days living at home, and you're an adult now. Success isn't coming easily. Songwriting is a passion but the road to becoming "famous," is difficult and rocky. You set your eyes on fame instead of writing solid material, but all that glitters doesn't seem to be real gold. You're constantly asking yourself questions about perseverance and confidence. Losing the fire you once had; becoming successful in the music industry seems almost obsolete.

Scenario Two: Your home life was filled with abuse and lack of support. Growing up, you had to fend for yourself and not rely on anyone else. Some days, you didn't know where your next meal would come from. The only thing you had was music and the ability to write. It's what kept you from going insane. You didn't know the first thing about songwriting, but you found books at the library on the subject because you couldn't afford to take music lessons. You began to write down goals for yourself to get out of your situation. As you begin to grow, you find a group of people who seem to have your interest at heart. They become your support team. Because of music; you've found a family. Each and every day, you work your hardest to succeed. You don't know any different—hard work has gotten you far. You have persevered through difficult times. Little successes begin to arise and still, you keep at it.

Out of those two scenarios; who would become the hit songwriter? Some of you would automatically choose one over the other. In reality; it's anyone's game. Becoming a hit songwriter isn't about gaining success quickly; it's about longevity in the field. Your physical environment can only hold you back for a time; then it's in your hands.

Mental Environment

Who's to say that your physical environment doesn't affect your mental environment? Think about a time when a teacher, parent, so-called friend said something hurtful to you. The statement sticks in your mind, and you replay it over and over again till you believe it. Even after you have shoved it out your brain; those words seem to come back and haunt you.

What about when you practice a riff for a tune or keep re-writing a verse to a song and you can't seem to be happy with what you are creating. The taunting begins. You're having this tug-of-war between what you know you have the potential to do and where you are at. Negative thoughts creep in and you begin to question your gift. Your emotions and mental environment reflect in your day to day activities and your craft.

Do you recall Henry Ford's saying, "Whether you think you can or think you can't, you're right,"? Sometimes all those negative, dark thoughts and encounters create fear--the type of fear that causes you to stop everything in its tracks. I call this being on the edge of "The Cliffs of Fear." We are right there—just about to step into a new world; a place where there is freedom in our craft but suddenly we are frozen. We see unknown territory and we have this fear of falling and not being able to pick

How Environment Plays a Role

ourselves up. In reality, we don't have a fear of failing. Failing is inevitable. Falling is frightening. Instead of trying and failing; we stand on that cliff wondering, "what if." Falling is far greater than failing. With failing, you tried; with being scared to fall—you didn't attempt at all. You're too afraid of the actual fall, not the outcome. Don't just stand on "The Cliffs of Fear," enjoy the view and let go of that negativity. Learn to have a healthy mental environment.

Motivation is crucial to our success in becoming a hit songwriter. We've all had people hurt us. Why do we focus on them? Why not think about those you help us when times are hard? The people who encourage and motivate us are the ones that should inspire us never to be afraid of falling because when we fail; they will be there for us. It takes one person to break us but it also takes one person to hold out their hand and walk through the journey to success with you. Think about how effective that is for your fear, mental state, craft, and success. One person can be the difference between your fear of falling and teaching you to fly.

Your environment can affect your success in songwriting, but you have to be motivated. Persevere through times that can seem like they will never get any better. Push yourself. Believe in your abilities. Surround yourself with positive and strong people.

Chapter Twenty-Five:

Interview with Psychotherapist and Author **Edy Nathan**

Psychotherapist and author, **Edy Nathan**

Edy Nathan, MA, LCSW is a licensed psychotherapist with over 20 years of experience specializing in the integration of psychotherapy and the world of spirituality. She holds a master's from New York University and Fordham. She has post-graduate training from the Ackerman Institute for Family Therapy, The Gestalt Center and the Jungian Institute.

Edy specializes in working with adults, couples and children. She holds 3-5-day intensive Grief To Grace and Growth groups in New York, Florida and New Jersey. She has been a Key Note Speaker and workshop leader for 9 years on the topic of Grief for the "Spiritual Healing Cruises" She has spoken for "The Thanatological Society" on "Grief Speak: Creative Ways to Cope with Loss." A leader in the field of grief she has spoken and led groups for "The Adoption Conference." At Beth Israel Hospital, where she worked intensely with long term illness, HIV/AIDS and Substance Abuse she was invited to speak at Grand Rounds about loss, speaking to patients about death and to staff on burnout in the workplace.

Do you believe drive, passion, and stamina (energy level) play a major role in helping a person to become a successful hit songwriter? If so, how?

Ambition, blind determination, an intuitive hustle, and unending cravings create some of the necessary layers needed to become a successful hit songwriter. The most important part of this recipe, however, is the ability to endure under duress, to find the resilience when meeting failure, and preserving the self through perseverance and a steadfast doggedness. Nothing stops them from the dream.

Do you think work ethic plays a vital part in becoming a hit songwriter? If so, how?

Is work ethic enough? Probably not. Working hard, painstakingly long hours doesn't make a successful hit songwriter. It's a combination of many internal and external experiences. Sometimes the push to become good, the unending rehearsals and rewrites keep a person in the same place. You must be willing to take a leap of faith and take the chances necessary to move into the realm of success.

How much does faith and belief in one's abilities help in becoming a hit songwriter?

Great to have the faith…it takes honest reflections on the self. Am I good? Where do I fail? What feedback am I getting? Is there enough feedback that is similar to give a more complete idea of how you are being received. Sometimes we are successful in our own minds, yet it doesn't mean we are tapping into something deep within others, something speaking to their psyches, something in the song that is part of a collective understanding at a primal level.

How much of focus to detail and perfection helps make a hit songwriter? Why?

Perfection. The Japanese say it's always good to have a crack in a pot to remind us there is no perfection. We are human and cannot really do anything perfectly.

Detail. There are many ways to manifest detail. It can become obsessive, which stops the action and ultimately stops production. It can be clumsy, like a who cares kinda attitude. Perhaps having a sense of organization. Knowing the goals, finding the ones which are reachable, and aligning the goals with the hunger and craving to become a successful songwriter.

What role does commitment to short and long-term goals affect success as a hit songwriter?

Creating a calendar of short and long term goals is part of success. It helps people heal through the tough times, while planning each step, each performance, the end game for each presentation, and what the next step will be. One goal leads to another, they enhance one another, they inform one another in big ways.

Do you believe that learning from failures and rejections help in becoming a hit songwriter? Please elaborate.

It's life, right? I used to have a friend who would say I can't wait to have 100 no's- because that means I'm that much closer to a yes. What you do with the failures and rejections is what contributes to becoming a hit songwriter. Write about the failure. Put into context. Ask yourself, not once, not twice, but many, many times- WHAT DID I LEARN HERE? How can I do this differently, better or with greater ease?

Do you feel like being obsessive and persistent with writing help in becoming a successful, hit songwriter? If so, how?

Obsessive behavior is like grief; it hangs around; it bothers you; it has its grasp on you and is relentless. There is a choice here. Use the anxiety within the obsessive behavior to get you in touch with your anger. Anger can be a great propeller for creativity. I'm not talking about the anger of outburst, rather the anger that is internal and yields a certain grace when it's honored.

Do you think taking risks in your career has helped you become successful? If so, how?

Definitely. I stopped thinking about why something couldn't work, and I just plowed through. No one would stop me, nothing would get in my way, and a "no" just meant I had to get to a yes! Living in NYC, office rents are high. My office had a window facing a wall, no light at all and it often felt as if I was in a prison. For reasons of sanity, I had to get out of the office, yet rents were unimaginably high. Taking a leap of faith, jumping into an office space that I could ill-afford, was what I did. This might not sound like a big deal- yet, this move changed the trajectory of my working life. The joy of having light, windows and personal space made all the difference in more than just my work life.

Do you believe having a positive mental attitude, being optimistic, and possessing a strong self-esteem play a major role in success? If so, how?

Strong self-esteem, able to take a hit whether artistically or in other arenas of one's life, is a huge part of success. Don't let the archetypal roles of the critic or the judge interrupt the process. The enemy who wants to put you down because of jealousy, contempt or fear can be your greatest teacher as long as you don't give them power. It is the power of self-esteem that the psyche needs for success.

Interview with Psychotherapist and Author **Edy Nathan**

Does being a doer and not a talker help in becoming successful? If so, how?

Why not both? Talk it and do it!!

Does being a visionary or a dreamer help artists become successful? If so, how?

Create a vision, live the dream and all things become possible. Without an image what is there?

Do you think overall personality contributes to the success of a songwriter? If so, how?

I'd love to say yes- but not necessarily.

Do you still continue to learn all you can about your profession? If so, how?

Absolutely! Keep learning, and it instills creativity, passion, and change. Think about the Beatles- they were always in states of metamorphosis, change, and conversion.

In any part of your life, has self-discipline played a major role in helping become successful? If so, how?

Yes, to be the best it takes a discipline like none other and a willingness to forgo temptations, so no matter what it takes: education, action and self-reflection, and loneliness to hear the cry within.

Do you believe a hit songwriter is born or made? Why?

Both. They can be born, and they can be made. Talent can certainly be innate, and yet, when facing the internal demons of life, those that tangle with the demons are often made into a greatness they might not have otherwise met.

Do you believe talent is a gift or is it earned? Explain your thoughts.

It is a gift. It is also earned. No matter. You may be born with talent, that's a gift. What you do with the talent is earned. How often have those famous folks who have been given the talent of artistry and yet have destroyed it?

What is talent?

Talent is the capacity to honor an internal endowment of soulful riches, genius and autonomous daring where chances are taken to expand a conversation that would not otherwise be available to the collective.

Do you believe self-criticism helps or harms the success of a hit songwriter? Explain.

Change the self-criticism by removing the self from blindness that keeps you stuck. Know the truth about who you are.

Do you believe hit songwriters are more attuned to what is going on and happening around them than others? Please elaborate.

Why would that be?

Do you believe inspiration is a state of mind and could it be a major factor in the creation of a hit songwriter? Why?

It is a state of mind, it is a state of being inspired and curious about the world, about people, about political conversations, and listening to what is being said around you. Getting the pulse of the dialogues happening in the world, being in silence, listening to your breath, and getting out of your comfort zone are all parts of inspiration and probably an essential element to being a hit songwriter.

Interview with Psychotherapist and Author **Edy Nathan**

Do you believe having empathy helps in becoming a hit songwriter? Explain.

What's the difference between empathy and compassion? Perhaps a bit of both is necessary. Tapping into the losses in one's life and owning them, knowing what brings you down and finding the light in the darkness and knowing you are not alone in this journey will help in this passage.

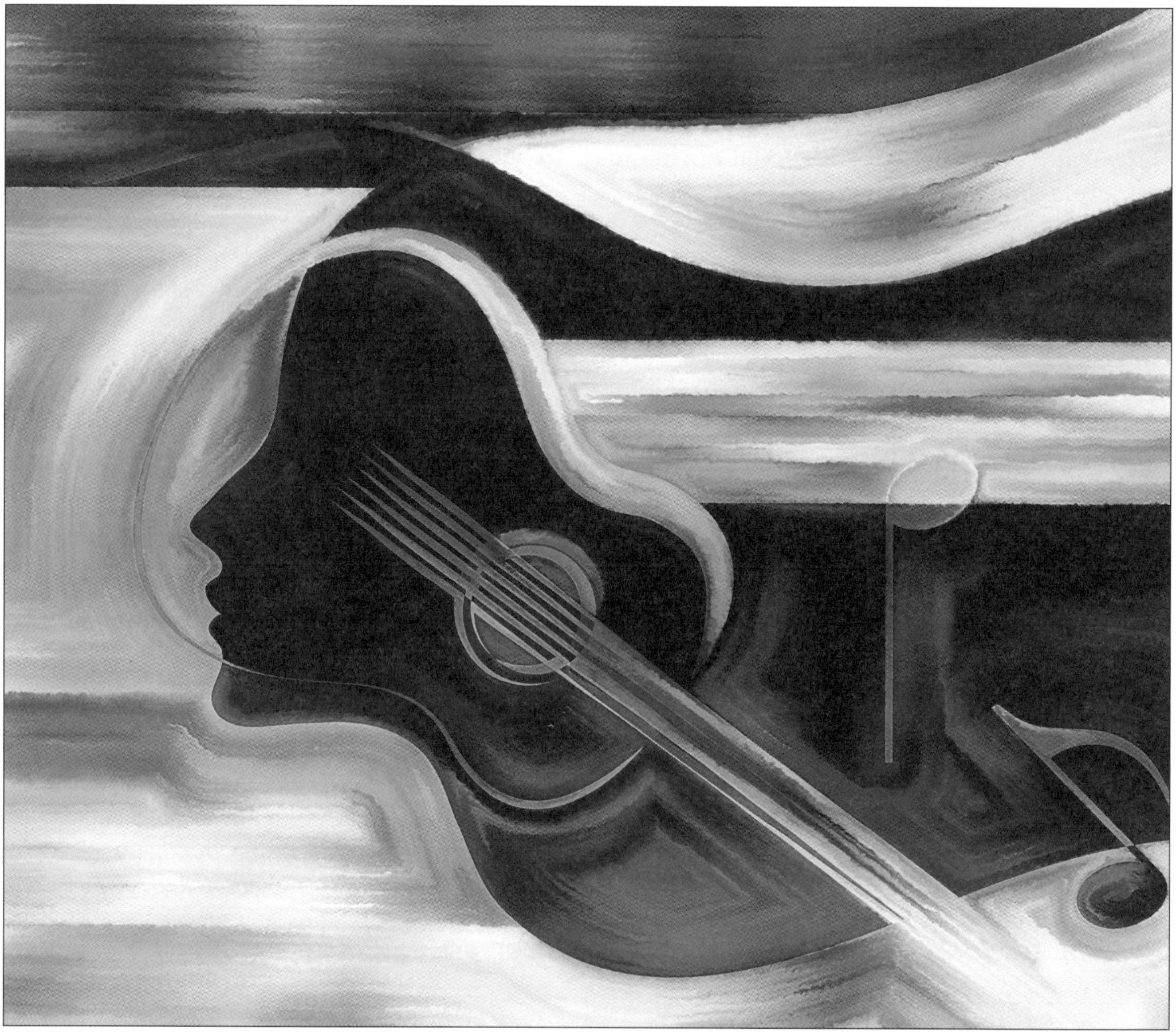

Chapter Twenty-Six:

Interview with Pediatrician **Dr. Jason Kastner**

Dr. Jason Kastner, pediatrician

Do you believe drive, passion, and stamina (energy level) play a major role in helping a person to become a successful hit songwriter?

Like many professions, there are often talented individuals that bring comparable skill sets to the table. What often sets others apart from the field is showing a drive, passion and endurance that surpasses others.

Do you think work ethic plays a vital part in becoming a hit songwriter? Is so, how?

The ability to go back to the drawing board over and over again, working tirelessly to pursue one's passion and get it "just right" is the mark of an outstanding artist. While never being a songwriter myself, I expect that cultivating a strong work ethic is a necessary ingredient in this ability as an artist.

How much does faith and belief in one's abilities help in becoming a hit songwriter?

Pursuing any dream, like becoming a successful songwriter must start with belief in one's self and abilities even when others don't share your same dream. The dream is what puts your talents and abilities into motion to bring the dream to life.

How much of focus to detail and perfection helps make a hit songwriter?

The artist owns the work. When it is exactly the work, they set out for it to be, in that authenticity and pursuit of perfection, there lies success.

What role does commitment to short and long-term goals affect success as a hit songwriter?

Like any dream that is bigger than ourselves, we should commit to short term goals that take us a little further each time along the journey rather than expecting overnight success in reaching the peak in the distance.

Do you believe that learning from failures and rejections help in becoming a hit songwriter? Please elaborate.

Learning to pick ourselves up after failure or rejection is the key to unlocking doors of opportunity. I would imagine that most hit songwriters can look back in their past and point to a failure that ultimately led to success.

Do you feel like being obsessive and persistent with writing help in becoming a successful hit songwriter? If so, how?

Interview with Pediatrician **Dr. Jason Kastner**

Obsessive is a strong word and, in my mind, a negative one. Persistence, on the other hand doesn't have to be obsessively all-consuming to the exclusion of other important aspects of life such as relationships and emotional and spiritual health.

Do you think taking risks in your career has helped you become successful? If so, how?

Most successful life and career stories involve taking some risk. And most people are risk-averse by nature. If it was easy, everyone would do it.

Do you believe having a positive mental attitude, being optimistic, and possessing strong self-esteem play a major role in success? If so, how?

Aside from helping give you the mental fortitude to succeed, especially in the face of adversity, a positive mind-set is contagious and attractional. What better way to get buy-in from others for your dream?

Does being a doer and not a talker help in becoming successful? If so, how?

Again, if it was easy, everyone would do it. The chasm between talking about doing something grand and actually setting out to do it is typically where the wheels come off.

Does being a visionary or a dreamer help artists become successful? If so, how?

Without a doubt. Like artwork, the fruit of a songwriter's labor is uniquely theirs. Their dream and their vision produce their masterpiece.

Do you think overall personality contributes to the success of a songwriter? If so, how?

I don't know this for certain, but I would expect the positively optimistic personality to find more success than the alternative.

Do you feel patience and practice play a role in the creation of a hit songwriter?

I do believe that patience is a must for anyone pursuing their dream. There is an element of being ready with "dream in hand" for just the right time.

How much prioritizing your life from day-to-day helps you become successful?

Time is the common denominator for all of us. Wasting too much of it on thoughts or activities that don't move us forward will ultimately rob us of what we hope for in the future we dream.

Do you continue to learn all you can about your profession? If so, how?

As a physician, I continue to learn how much I really have to learn. Maintaining a posture of being an active learner is what keeps us fresh and enjoying the purpose this life has given us.

In any part of your life, has self-discipline played a major role in helping become successful? If so, how?

Self-discipline starts with the small things and is the inoculation that helps us tackle the big things. Getting up early to start the day ahead of schedule allows us the flexibility to take on the bigger tasks that require our time and energy.

Is there any factor, trait, or ingredient we may have omitted that helps in becoming a successful, hit songwriter?

I can't think of any.

Do you believe a hit songwriter is born or made? Explain your thoughts.

Clearly, there is a good portion of talent and ability

that is innately given and imprinted into each of us. Discovering that, cultivating it through hard work and pursuing it with passion is when a "star is (actually) born."

Do you believe talent is a gift or is it earned? Explain your thoughts.

Talent is gifted to us by our Creator. What we do with that is up to us.

Do you believe that talent comes from within? If so, is it how they process stimuli in life?

Ditto above.

What is talent?

That unique excellence that lies in each of us.

Do you believe self-criticism helps or harms the success of a hit songwriter?

The artist is often his/her worst critic and because they own the resulting product, it can only help drive them to produce that which bears their unique mark.

Do you believe hit songwriters are more attuned to what is going on and happening around them than others?

My observation is that they are typically more intro- and extro-spective than others. I think that is a good thing when dealing with creative people.

Chapter Twenty-Seven:

Interview with **Dr. Denise Stuart, MD**

Pediatrician, **Denise Stuart, MD**

Dr. Denise Stuart received her medical degree from Saint Louis University in 2001 and completed her Pediatric residency at the University of Florida in Jacksonville, Florida in 2004. She received board certification in 2004 from the American Board of Pediatrics. She practices Pediatric Medicine just outside of Nashville in Hendersonville, TN. She has two young violinists at home training in the Suzuki method.

Conclusive Paragraph:

One of the great things about spending time with children is watching them develop over the years into unique individuals. When I discuss their interests and activities every year at well-child exams, I can see students of music training enjoying growth in that skill set year after year. They may start with individual lessons, but then age into a time of more collaborative organized groups. From jam sessions with friends, to middle school bands, to junior symphonies there are opportunities to continue to develop their talents. They learn to become more creative, to practice persistence, and to problem solve as individuals and a group. Remarkably, music is the one activity most adolescent children tell me they rely on in times of emotional need. And it is gift that they can share with others and still enjoy as adults.

Do you think taking risks in your career has helped you become successful? If so, how?

I would have to agree with this statement. I think it is vital to actively seek opportunities as we develop in our careers. We don't know where it may lead which implies a risk. But taking risks help us grow and ultimately is what adds to our success.

Do you believe having a positive mental attitude, being optimistic, and possessing a strong self-esteem play a major role in success? If so, how?

Certainly, there must be level of belief in order to achieve. The work can be done, but if you don't believe in yourself, it will be much harder for other's to as well. I have the honor in my career in medicine to have the faith of others placed in me every day. Acknowledging that makes it possible to stay optimistic through whatever challenges come.

Does being a doer and not a talker help in becoming successful? If so, how?

Dreaming and imagining are fantastic jumping points for creativity. But you still must jump! Taking action or making it happen require more practice and planning. The doing must take over the talking.

Interview with **Dr. Denise Stuart, MD**

Does being a visionary or a dreamer help artists become successful? If so, how?

Certainly, to create something which is perhaps new is probably easier for the dreamer. He or she may need to use that same creative insight to form a path to achieve it. It may take visionary skills to bring something to fruition.

How much prioritizing your life from day-to-day helps you become successful?

There must be priorities to reach accomplishment. There are seemingly endless tasks each day to complete. Most of what we do appears immediate in need. But we must have time carved out for the goals of tomorrow, next week, next month, or next year and beyond. In my career, the immediate task of caring for my patients on a work day takes priority. But there is always another priority being worked on which is my continuing education to improve my skills and knowledge. The longer-term goal is to keep learning and improving. The big picture must be kept in mind continually.

Do you continue to learn all you can about your profession? If so, how?

Absolutely. Keeping up-to-date with current recommendations, treatments, and care are vital to my success and my patient's health. In the medical profession, it involves reading, attending conferences, and meeting, and conferring and collaborating with colleagues.

Do you believe talent is a gift or is it earned? Explain your thoughts.

I have the unique experience of watching many children grow up. I would say their talents seem to rise as equally from a gift, as from passion. In the early years, I think it's best described as a natural inclination met with desire. At some point, there is a choice to cultivate it or not and from there forward, it has to be earned.

Chapter Twenty-Eight:
Broken Dreams

Sometimes, as hard as one tries, a dream doesn't always become reality. And while we only devoted one chapter to this negative aspect of songwriting, we must also face the fact that some people will never succeed in the career of songwriting as professionals. But our focus in the entire book is on the positivity, not the negatively of songwriting, while at the same time we must be realistic.

There are just too many songwriters, the odds are stacked against the songwriters, and the field is so competitive that it would be impossible for everyone to make it on a professional level. There are only so many artists and so many positions on the top of the charts. It seems like today; songwriting has become more difficult than it used to be. Many artists are writing their own songs without outside songwriters. Many groups are self-contained and cliquish, meaning one artist writes with a group of writers and producers under one roof and there is no room for any outside writers. Many artists today are self-contained packages. The producer has spent much time and energy developing that artist. The producer brings in the top hit songwriters he or she wishes to write with the artist. Since the music industry has changed with little money being made from the sale of albums-CD's and money being lost from streaming and pirating, the producer makes up for the lost revenue by keeping everything in-house: the publishing, writers, artist, production, engineers, musicians all under one roof. It is difficult or almost impossible for the independent or new songwriter to break into that clique. Songwriting can be political, meaning it's who you know and work with. I have been booked months in advance with some well-known hit songwriters only to be canceled at the last minute because that hit songwriter had the opportunity to write with the latest, hot new artist who was in town.

According to *The Tennessean,* 100 new songwriters move to Nashville as well as other music industry cities, and while many are still new and learning their craft, it does make the talent pool highly competitive. You can seem to do all the right things and still not succeed. Many wise hit songwriters say it takes anywhere from seven to 10 years to become a country hit songwriter in Nashville. I am sure Los Angeles, London, and New York hit songwriters would give the same advice. But not all songwriters make it even after trying diligently for seven to 10 years. You can do all the writer nights, network with all the right people, co-write with everyone in town to learn your craft, join NSAI, TSA, The Songwriter's Guild and NARAS, AFM, write six to eight hours a day, even sign with a publisher as a staff writer, and still not make it as professional songwriter.

To understand the odds that are stacked against songwriters, one hit songwriter told me it is easier to be elected a United States senator than have a top 10, *Billboard*-charted song. Now those are some odds.

Bart Herbison, Executive Director of the Nashville Songwriters Association International, tells it like it is in his comments about the almost-impossible odds for songwriters: "I don't have any statistical analysis to show, some study the city of Nashville did. But right now, my best projection is there's probably 80,000 people in Nashville that will tell you they are here to become a successful songwriter, or artist, or engineer or in some creative aspect of music. Truth be known, maybe 8,000 of those would have any modicum of talent that would ever result in that dream coming truth. Truth be known, maybe 800 have the wherewithal and the resilience to go through the trials and errors and the years it takes to make it. And probably only 80 ever make it to the extent of knowing anything they did. Those are hefty odds. And those were the people who moved here to do it. Those are the people who were probably the stars in their hometown."

I can tell you first-hand how frustrating the business can be. Just when you think you are on the verge of making it, you get humbled or set back by various roadblocks that keep you from advancing or discourage you in some way. You might receive word that some hot new artist has a hold on your song, or that the artist will be cutting your song. That has happened to me many times. The producer, record label and publisher led me to believe my recorded song would make the album only to find out later; my song was pushed off the album by a last-minute pitched song which was recorded by that artist. I have also had well-known, and new artists call me and swear they would be recording one of my songs. They absolutely loved the song and promised me they would be recording it, only to learn later they had either lost interest in the song or had forgotten about me. It's a fickle business. You must have thick skin and never take anything personally. You must let everything roll off your back. Remember, it's a business. I would love to trust everyone in this world. But unfortunately, in the music business, it's hard to believe a word anyone tells you, it's not like some tangible professions and occupations where someone's word is their bond. The music business changes with the wind. I am not sure exactly why it is so unpredictable, perhaps because the supply is greater than the demand. Maybe because the competition is so stiff. One minute, the producers or artists can be super excited about your tune and are ready to record it until they discover another song which catches their ears even stronger than your tune. This phenomenon can happen within a matter of seconds. I've witnessed a monster hit being bumped as a radio single for another song which was suddenly pitched at the very last minute. And today, producers and record companies are not recording albums, but are recording and releasing one single at a time with artists.

While you are working hard to succeed as a songwriter, you must provide some income to pay the bills, which at the same time allows you enough freedom and time to write songs. Therefore, it is important to find work which pays the maximum amount per hour, so you don't spend your whole life working on a "money gig." Performance gigs for weddings and special events which pay hourly rates of $50 or more are a good start. Private coaching and teaching usually pay upwards of $40 an hour and can be achieved with a computer setup in your place via Skype or Facetime. You can coach or teach anyone in the world. And best of all, you can set your own hours. Find a hobby or skill you know best and put it to good use making money part-time while you are working to achieve your songwriting dream. If you were to work at teaching or performing 15 to 20 hours a week at $40 an hour, that would be equivalent to $600 to $800 a week or $2400 to $3200 a month which should be enough to pay the bills if living single and frugally. That would give you anywhere from six to eight hours a day to concentrate on writing, recording, pitching, and networking. This would be an efficient use of time instead of working a full 40-hour-week job where you would be tired and worn out. There would be little time to devote to songwriting if you had to work five or six full days or nights per week. The secret is to work fewer hours and earn the maximum amount per hour.

Broken dreams don't just occur through not achieving your songwriting dreams. I've seen songwriters who have lost their husbands or wives to divorces or broken relationships with their boyfriends or girlfriends. The struggling songwriter commitment is hard on relationships. If you don't have a very supportive spouse or a boyfriend-girlfriend who thoroughly understands the music business and what you are going through, you run the risk of losing that person in a relationship. A serious songwriter devotes countless hours to the business. Many spouses or boyfriend-girlfriends feel neglected or threatened by the business and how much time it consumes the songwriter.

Many times, aspiring songwriters find themselves in a quandary. They have bills to pay, so they work hard, but seem to never find enough time to write songs. It is a frustrating situation to be in. Unfortunately, many songwriters get so involved in their "money gigs" that they lose track of the reason they first came to Nashville, Los Angeles or New York. They get so wrapped up in working, paying bills and into life. Next thing you know, they find themselves doing something completely different than what they planned on doing. They have lost all sense of their purpose for moving to a city to become a songwriter. One day they wake up and find they are no longer a songwriter. That is sad, but a reality. I have witnessed this scenario time and time again with people I have known over the years.

There are people I've known who have come to Nashville and have become very successful as hit songwriters. They have overcome all the odds. These people are few and far between, but despite all the odds against songwriters, it is still possible to be successful. There are many broken dreams, but out of the pile of broken pieces, there are some very successful, hit songwriters who rise above it all.

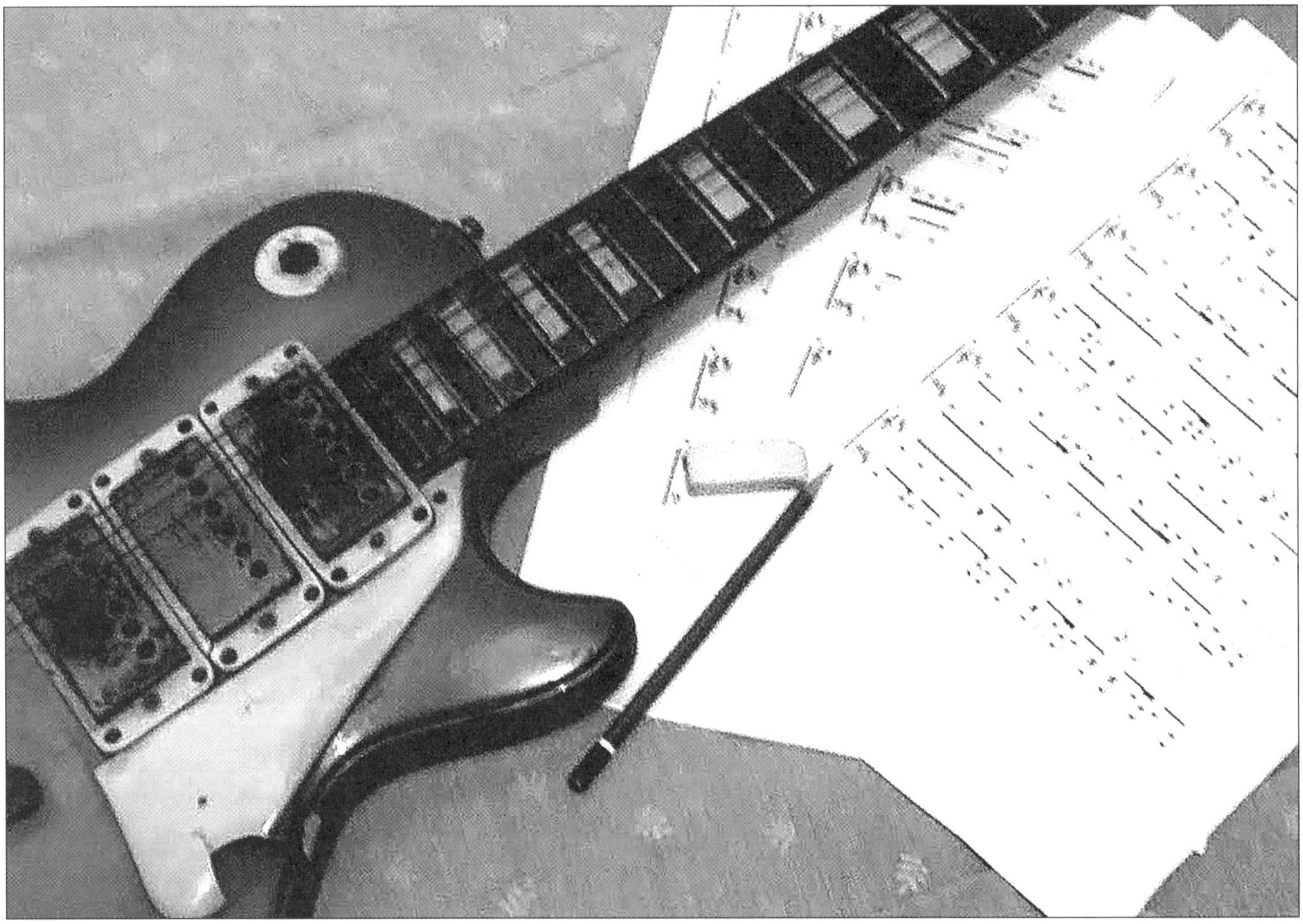

Chapter Twenty-Nine:

Summary of Findings Through Research and Interviews

It has been an honor to interview such talented, gifted and distinguished participants for this book. We have been inspired beyond belief by reading the interviews of 20 hit and legendary songwriters, eight producers, five recording artists, three songwriting coaches, two pediatricians, one psychologist, one music business attorney, and the Executive Director of the Nashville Songwriters Association International. We sincerely hope the interviews, research, and conclusions will inspire you as it has for us. This book has influenced and moved us closer to searching for and achieving greatness. We are grateful to our publisher and to all those who participated in the writing of this book.

First, we learned from the interviews and research that drive and passion play an important role in becoming a hit songwriter. Everyone we interviewed stressed the significance of drive and passion. We received the following comments: "it is driven by a deep desire," "how bad do you want it?", "you have to do it 24/7", and that passion and drive is the "driving force" to becoming successful as a hit songwriter. Other comments were: "everyone is born with passion", "need deep desire to express yourself musically", "stamina and patience are important", "need thick skin", "need to risk it all without a safety net (no plan b or career choice to fall back on)", "you have to get out there and pound the pavements—more so than ever", "you have to be an all-in-one, do-it-yourself person", "you must have an unquenchable fire in your belly to do this songwriting thing", "the only difference between a hit songwriter and one that doesn't succeed is they give up", "the people who love it the most think about it all the time", "no room for part- time writers or talkers", " I've seen a lot of talented people leave this town (Nashville) because they didn't persevere long enough", and "you work hard, you can't conceive to writing a song in one day and letting it go, without looking at it the next day, and maybe the day after that, and the day after that."

After all the interviews and reading the above comments, we wondered why anyone would want to try their hand at such a difficult, risky career as songwriting if they didn't have deep passion and drive. If they didn't have a deep love for songwriting and didn't want to write 24/7 without making any money, why would they want to continue in it? Perhaps they want to write songs for the wrong reasons: fame, money, attention, etc. All of that might come to you in your lifetime, but the real reason most songwriters write is because they have a passion for it and would do it 24/7 even if they made no money from it. It is true; however, this is called the music business, and we must also write songs that will sell and move people's feelings.

Next, we discovered that work ethic plays a major role in becoming a successful hit songwriter. Everyone we interviewed agreed that work ethic was vital except for one songwriter. That songwriter has seen major hit songwriters who were laid-back and didn't appear to work very hard. Go figure. We received the following comments: "you must write even if you don't feel like it", "you need to set aside time every day whether it be one hour or eight hours", "you need to put in the hours", "everyone has their own work ethic", and "it's not just about writing songs, but putting in the hours demoing, networking and pitching the songs."

Additional comments were received on work ethic were: "it is a balance, "everybody's work ethic is different," "some people are more laid back than others", " it takes writing a ton of bad songs for every good one", "don't wait for the inspiration, start working at writing", "work ethic is about how many times you get back up", "it's another way of describing discipline," "going back to the drawing board over and over again", "working tirelessly to pursue one's passion and to get it "just right" is the mark of an outstanding artist", "Is work ethic enough? Probably not. You must be willing to take a leap of faith and take the chances necessary to move into the realm of success", "whatever makes you successful in anything will make you successful as a songwriter as long as you have that gift", " I find the more successful songwriters over the long term know the American songbook over the decades, and they know generations of songs", "If you're going to be a staff songwriter writer you have to have good ethics and be very disciplined.", "it is essential," "Again, no matter how hard you work, how hard your work ethic is, you still must have, inside you, some degree of talent and ability.", " I'm a believer in work ethic, if it's me, getting to the keyboard every day, if I can do that, just to play. If I come up with something great, if I don't come up with something, it's a process. You do not win every day."

On the faith and belief question, we found that it is very important to have confidence in yourself as a songwriter. Some of the opinions we received were: "there is a fine line between arrogance and confidence," "very important," "blind faith is putting it out there into the universe," "confidence is the key" and "if you believe you can, you can." One writer suggested that others gravitate toward confident people who believe 1000% in themselves. So, optimism and confidence are super important even if others don't show the same confidence in you.

Additional opinions on faith and belief were: "I don't believe in perfection, I am a big picture person," " A song you listen to on the radio either washes over you or makes you feel something.", "When you go back and look at the most successful songs and their lyrics, at least 70 to 80% of those lyrics are unintelligible.", "Faith comes from a higher source.", "There are many, many "haters" and "bullies" trying to bring others down. One must not listen to all that negativity but have faith and belief in themselves to keep the strength and the dream and to keep moving always forward.", "Faith and belief are everything.", "I believe insecurity can be an artist's motivation to succeed because it sucks to be insecure.", "always have to believe God made you and you must believe you are here for a purpose," "Well, you do build faith in yourself when you get a degree of acceptance; when you find a song you really liked got recorded by such and such an artist; you find acceptance for yourself when the song goes on and becomes a top-10 hit, give yourself six days. Go to your instrument, sit. You get nothing. Don't get discouraged. I've gone three days, and I've gotten nothing. Chalk it up to a good day even if you get nothing. You don't get to that point unless you stick with it. Don't get discouraged. It's a hard game. It has always been hard."

It appears, from our interviews and research, that having faith and belief go a long way in helping a person to become a hit songwriter. Optimism is a great gift and trait to have as a songwriter.

When we asked about focus to detail and perfection, we learned most songwriters agree that detail and perfection help make a hit songwriter as long as it doesn't affect the feel or emotions of the song. Some of the remarks received were: "one little note, or change in production can change everything", "make sure everything is right in a song", "let go of perfection for emotions instead", "no songs are perfect, not even on the radio", "create to perfection." Not every songwriter was sold on the use of detail and perfection in writing songs.

Some felt it was a detriment. A few writers thought it kept a songwriter from expressing his or her emotions in a song. Others felt a songwriter could perfect a song so much that he or she could either get to the point of diminishing returns with the song or that he or she would never finish the song due to constantly perfecting it. A comment pertaining to this, "some songwriters beat it to death and never finish a song."

More views from songwriters were the

following: "Songs are always a work in progress," "always tweaking," "There's a fine line between making it perfect and communicating with the listeners.", "The song will tell you what it wants and needs if you're listening.", "Focus on the message first, then go over it again with attention to detail.", "Focus and detail are immensely important.", "I don't believe there is really any such thing as "perfection," "We are all imperfect.", "I go back after writing the song to see if the essence of that person is in there and if the poignancy or sadness of them has been painted well enough.", "I've had songs which took a year to write and others that took 30 minutes to write, when you know what you want to say, it just comes.", "Focus to detail is a must, but some of the best art is accidental and trying to perfect it is essentially impossible.", "We are human beings and cannot really do anything perfect.", "Words matter in songwriting.", "So little details, attention to what makes a song special and different are essential, especially if you're going to have a long-term career of this songwriting.", "Songwriting is a craft and a skill.", "Careful attention to how you build and perfect that song is important—just like building a house.", "I have always been pretty picky about my lyrics.", " I've never had success at anything, looking back at it, that I didn't have fun with it. When you're having fun is when your creativity is the best.", " I think it's hard to be consistently excellent and successful at anything challenging without an obsessive attention to the fine points.", and "I think some of the details towards making a song good, or were acceptable for me, were getting away from my instrument, the keyboard, sitting on the couch, sitting in a chair, hearing it in my head instead of hearing it at the piano, or the synthesizer or whatever it be. Because when you're sitting at the keyboard, you are getting it bar-by-bar, you don't hear the longevity of that song from the start to finish. I think that is the very key. I think it is important for young songwriters to be able to--instead of dumping their ideas on a phone, I am much in favor that they do that, but they also are able to, if they are on a plane and have a cocktail napkin, to write out not just the lyric, but the actual melody because they hear it in their heads."

Most of the songwriters agreed that short and long-terms were helpful and necessary in achieving success as a hit songwriter. One writer felt like some goals songwriters set were unrealistic. He said, "some goals are beyond our control," Short-term and long-term goals are important for songwriters as long as they set reachable goals possibly in small steps or set realistic goals.

Some additional remarks were: "Short or long term--always commit to it.", "Commitment could also be called madness.", "Be deliberate about making lists of your goals, hanging them up where you can see them daily and marking them off as you reach them.", "Have a one-year plan and a five-year plan.", "I've always believed in the long-term goal, but the way to get there is the short-term goals in between.", "Goals are good to have, but I believe flexibility is key as goals are constantly changing and getting derailed.", "Commitment truly affected my success.", "Best short-term goal I know of is a deadline.....long term goal...make enough money to retire.", "I think the goal is the song every day—to get up and do something that's going to make somebody feel something." "You must be present to win, so you gotta get up and believe that today is the day I might have that magic song.", "Throw out the short-term thing because you can go a year without getting a song to an artist you want to get it to. You could wait on an artist for four years, and then he might change his mind or her mind and record the song. It requires patience. It's not an overnight thing. You can write a song and have the artist like it and have the record company, not like it."

Whether it be short or long-term goals, most songwriters made use of them.

Every songwriter thought learning from failure and rejections was most important to the process of becoming a hit songwriter, provided the songwriter used the failure and rejections as a learning tool to achieve future success. Here are some of the comments we received: "once you make a mistake, you are less likely to make the same mistake again," and "failures make you stronger." But one writer said he rejected "rejection" and said, "you have to define failure." He continued by saying, "some of my songs are great songs, but they never became hits." The writer said that "rejection" is only one person's opinion. It doesn't mean the song isn't a hit. Nevertheless, failure and rejection seem to play a major part in helping songwriters learn to become successful.

Other opinions about failure and rejection were: "How do you define failure?", "Mistakes are great teachable moments.", "What is failure? If you can't take failure, you're in the wrong business, no matter what you do.", "learning from rejection," "Failure and success are very subjective and relative.", "My mother convinced me to do things that I wasn't even capable of, and so it was impossible for anyone to convince me otherwise or that I was worthless.", "Ask yourself "what did I learn here?", "Failure is the greatest teacher.", "The last thing a professional wants to hear is constant praise.", "I would say it's learning that is a part of the process.", "Failure means you tried. Without trying, then you wouldn't have received an answer.", "I prefer not to use the words "failures "and "rejections.", "I think of them as a process of elimination, taking me one step further to success.", "There is a fine line between failure and rejection.", "A lot of times when you're rejected, it doesn't mean you're a failure.", "I believe in the incremental approach, in building something, which is usually a gradual process." , "You know, I've written some songs that I thought were really good—worthy of being heard, worthy of being possible hits. You're not the decider there. You may think they are worthy, and they think they're not worthy. Works the other way too—someone else says, "No, I really believe in the song." "Don't forget, when you're writing the song, and you're really spending some time with the song, it's a short form, not a long form, three minutes of telling a story with a good melody; and if you write like the way I write, which is hearing it hundreds of times in different forms."

Most of the songwriters agreed that being obsessive and persistent were necessary in becoming a successful, hit songwriter. Here are their views on this subject: "I am obsessive about songwriting.", "I don't think being obsessive is healthy.", "Yes, you have to be obsessive about everything in writing.", "Obsession is another word for passion.", "It takes obsession and persistence to get good at anything.", "I prefer self-discipline to obsession.", "A great writer is a complete human being." , "Obsessive, no. I don't think that serves one well overall." "Persistent" yes.", "Everyone works differently; I find it works best for me if I'm just inspired by something real. I'm not one of those people that can sit down and make myself write.", "The more I learned, the more I knew I needed to learn.", "Obsessive is a strong word, and in my mind a negative one. Persistence, on the other hand, doesn't have to be obsessively, all time consuming to the exclusion of the other important aspects of life such as relationships and emotional and spiritual health.", "Obsessive behavior is like grief; it hangs around, it bothers you.", "I hold songwriters akin to great painters. It's almost an obsessive, dysfunctional, beautiful, wonderful gift all wrapped up into the same juxtaposed things that come together.", "The more you do it, the better you get.", "I pitched my song 124 times before it was cut 10 times.", "You must write a lot of songs to get that one hit song." and "It's easier for me because I can take a long time to write stuff; I am very obsessive about it: would it be better this way or would it be better that way, compulsive about it.... a lot of composers go into a song they want to become a hit. But the moment of truth for me is where it goes once when it leaves my hands and goes into a studio with an arranger writing an arrangement, an A & R man with a vocal with the musicians playing, what the orchestration sounds like, what the tempo feels like. There are a lot of things unless you're the producer yourself, you don't have control of. I think I had a certain amount of songs early on in my career that maybe got ruined in somebody's else's hands —the arranger, the A & R man, the choice of artist to sing the song, the tempo of it. You have to acknowledge that it is a set operation for me."

Many of the songwriters, producers, and artists we interviewed have taken risks in their careers. Some have played it safe and felt uncomfortable taking risks. Those who said they had taken risks attributed their risk-taking to the successes they had achieved. Here are some of the opinions on the topic of taking risks: "Experiment with a song, and it might become number one.", "If you're not a risk taker forget about trying to be a pro songwriter.", "It's risky being a songwriter; it's risky being a musician or anything in the arts.", "I'm not a huge risk taker." "It doesn't happen in the shallow end of the pool.", "I believe any time I have said "yes" and took a risk, it has helped for sure.", "I think risks are necessary for growth and accomplishments." Yes, I have taken risks and have succeeded.", "It's sink or swim.", "Most successful life and career stories involve taking some risk.", "Taking risks can change everything in your life.", "I find the songwriters who will occasionally take a risk; those tend to be some of your biggest songs.", "I prefer taking calculated risks sometimes, instead of saying "taking risks.", "I say I'm going to be bold. If you are constantly careful, and never be bold, your answer will always be "no.", " I definitely think that if I hadn't taken a risk, I wouldn't have gone down the path I went.", and "If you play it too safe you will not be successful."

Most of those interviewed said it helped to have a positive mental attitude, to be optimistic, and to possess strong self-esteem. Most agreed those qualities and traits play a major role in songwriting success. Two songwriters differed in their opinions. One said, "Songwriters have this weird duality of a complete lack of self-esteem, none whatsoever, while they are some of the most confident people that have ever lived 100%." And another said, "Yes, but many people with low self-esteem and an enormous amount of self-doubt succeed."

The majority of songwriters said the following: "You've got to be grateful for the process of making the music (enjoying the moment) that experience and never take it for granted," "Positivity, optimism, and good self-esteem are attractive things and assets to the successful songwriter.", "Confidence is very important.", "You need a good amount of self-esteem that nobody can break down.", "If you're lucky enough to be born with all three in your DNA, then yes it helps enormously.", "A positive mindset is contagious and attractional.", "Strong self-esteem is a huge part of success.", "If you are negative, your whole body is affected. Your songs won't be any good, and they will be the same over and over again." "You must act like you know what you're doing even if you don't know what you're doing.", "Yes, that's back to faith and hope," and "Success brings success. When you have a hit, your self-esteem goes up. You go a year without getting anything recorded or anything published, and it affects self-esteem, sure."

Most of those interviewed said it was important to "do" and not "talk." Here are some of the comments from hit songwriters: "So many people call themselves writers and never write anything.", "I'm all about doing and not talking—just do it.", "Talking with nothing behind it--should be a salesman for used cars, you shouldn't be in the music business.", "What you do is the statement of your quality.", "One is reliable if they are a "doer" and get the job done.", "Someone who is willing to walk the walk and do it—there are no excuses in their conversations.", "All talk and no walk rarely work, but still has to do some amount of self-promotion.', "You still must jump.", "The doing must take over the talking," "Why not both, talk it and do it!", "You have to be a doer.", "You have to get up and write every day.", "It is a volume exercise.", "I think talking about it helps, but then strap on your boots and get to work.", "By the mere act of doing, they are telling me they are serious, and I can count on working with them--they are not flaking.", "I think it was Fred Foster who said, "if you have to tell me how great the song is, then it's probably not that great of a song." , and "You've got to put the time in. You've got to make it like you're going into the office. Basically, the best rule, though I don't do it every day, I should do it every day; the goal is to go to the office every day. And maybe come up with nothing—that's okay. Maybe you have a lyric you've been working on, you try it again. Spend the time, look at it another way, get away from the keyboard, sit in a chair, listen to it in your head. You see it helps for me that I can go into the studio, and know how the rhythm section will be playing, and know how to translate that song in my head and in my heart-where the strings come in, or where the strings don't come in, or if they're strings at all, where someone's singing out of tune, where there should be harmony...I mean, these are things that you live and the record lives or dies by your decisions."

Those who were asked if being a visionary or a dreamer helped songwriters become successful, we got a mixed reaction of opinions: "Visionaries are on a different level, thinking in ways and creating something no one has done before.", "You need to be a dreamer to create.", "Yes, but very few will understand vision or your dream.", "I tend to be a visionary in writing.", "Create a vision, live the dream, and all things become possible.", "Without an image, what is there.?", "Dream that you can do this.", "I think we all start off as a dreamer-- we visualize ourselves winning some big award and even go as far as writing our acceptance speech. If you do that, then you know how much work, you have to do to get there.", "Yes, it helps to visualize the act of success.", and "I don't think you can say you're going to be visionary—it either will happen or it won't. You just do the best you can in writing the best you are able to write. Put the visionary in the drawer. Let someone else make that decision or whether you're a visionary."

Some writers cited the many different personalities of songwriters. Some said the personality of the writer didn't matter. Others begged to differ. Most agreed they enjoyed being with nice, kind and friendly people. Here are some of the opinions received: "Be nice, be professional, and respectful—leave your ego at the door.", "The best writers are chameleons, assuming whatever personality necessary to best deliver the story they need to tell.", "so many different types of personalities in this business," "I don't think it matters unless it's an overwhelmingly negative one, or egotistical or narcissistic.", "We all have different personalities in all aspects of life.", "I think we can only be true to ourselves and be who we are.", "I think good social skills are imperative in life.", "Thanking people goes a long way, it pays to be friendly.", "I believe personality has little to do with the creative process.", "Much of the most beautiful and important music has been created by grumpy people.", "not necessarily," "Yes, personality contributes.", "There are very successful people in the world who aren't the nicest.", "Being kind, courteous, respectful and nice to others goes a long way.", " Being grateful helps.", "Yes, being basically a friendly person with integrity makes a big difference particularly in the long run.", and "I think personality enters into the picture when it is a collaborative effort-two writers working on a song instead of just one writer. If two writers happen "to get along" who's not budging, and who's not threatened, who feels overwhelmed or who is doing the overwhelming themselves. It' not fair. It's better if you leave your ego at the door. If you write with someone you've never written with before and you think you won't get anything, you won't get anything or will get something. Better to begin with an open mind and at best, certainly get along.

All of those interviewed felt patience and practice played a role in the creation of a hit songwriter. Their remarks concerning this topic were: " Take your time and be patient--sometimes the great ones don't come to you right away.", "Practice: if you want to succeed as a writer, keep writing, keep working at getting better.", "Patience is probably the thing that is in least supply of every person I know.", "Most songwriters are not patient with themselves.", "Patience is very much a vocation of "hurry up and wait.", "Songwriters are always endlessly waiting.", "Depends on the song you're writing, yes." "There is the element of being ready with "Dream in hand" for just the right time.", "Definitely, practice is essential.", "Patience is a requirement.", "You definitely have to have patience because things move very slowly around here.", " Indisputably, patience, sadly things move at their own pace, not at mine..", and "Totally…you have to have patience, you can't give up on something. If you go three days and you still haven't gotten the bridge of a song, then you look at it another way. You try it another way you go about that bridge. You don't just throw the song away just because you don't have the right bridge."

Most songwriters agreed that prioritizing your life from day-to-day helps you become successful hit songwriter. Their remarks support this statement: "Time management is very, very important—too many distractions today living in the digital world.", "You have to say, "here's what I want to accomplish today. Here are my priorities." "It is the most important thing." , "Organizing your day to write and work is important.", "You can prioritize and plan all you want, but most days some things come along that that rearrange our priority list.", "Being flexible and not too rigid to a schedule is a great thing.", "You've got to get your life in order before you can write songs.", "I think your priority is to write as much as possible, but I also know you could burn yourself out..", and "I don't think I had any talent when I started. I have talent now, so that's come. You just see how things evolve. You have success; then you have more success. But you 're still not totally sure if you've got it all; if you're terrific, or rare and good, or pretty good.; you don't take anything for granted."

When those interviewed were asked if they continued to learn all they could about their profession, all of them had a thirst for knowledge about the music business and had a desire to stay current with their songwriting. Here are their comments: "Keep learning to stay in touch with what's contemporary.", "Check out the top 30 songs in the Hot 100 at *Billboard*.com. Look at the songs, why are they hits? How did they end up on the charts? How many songwriters wrote each song and how are they structured?", "The greatest university in the world is right there in your car, or your iPhone or on Spotify.", "If you're not continuing to learn and grow in your life in general and your profession specifically, you're atrophying.", "Always learning.", "It's amazing how much this profession is changing every day.", "I think everybody that is good and wants to be good is always trying to learn.", "I continue to be inspired by good songwriters and players, but not enough to steal from them.", "They inspire me enough to broaden my horizons.", "studying other hit songs," "I'm an advocate for songwriters. Every two years there's a new Congress to get to know.", "I'm constantly learning people in songwriting can be quite approachable, especially if you have the great desire to learn." , "If a songwriter gets really hot, I'll listen to 7 or 8 of their songs and try to see what they are doing." and "You learn about life, you stay open. You don't stay closed. It's all about living—doing what you see and what you feel. Basically, if you're open, you write who you are. If you've got talent, all the better. And if you're not -so-talented, you still write who you are. If it's a true, honest picture of how you're feeling, and how you're approaching it. That, to me, gives you the power."

Most all those interviewed cited self-discipline as a major contributor to their success as hit songwriters. Self-discipline is an admirable trait and quality to possess. These are the interviewer's remarks on self-discipline: "Yes, self-discipline plays a big part.", "Yes, self--discipline is the foundation of a successful songwriter.", "Yes, I am quite balanced and focused and disciplined and able to work under very stressful conditions," "It 's, and I had to be self-disciplined to not throw in the towel.", "Self-discipline starts with the small things and is the inoculation that helps us tackle the big things.", "The single biggest career killer, besides not having your life in order, is (suppose you become a professional) is not showing up .", "I like to think of it as "willingness to work" rather than "you have to work.", "Yes, I don't take writing lightly. I don't throw it away, I mean if a song doesn't work out. It took me three weeks to write the melody of Alfie to Hal's lyrics. It's a kind of discipline and obsessiveness. You know, I'm pretty good at that stuff—being obsessive about it—some things and tempos."

When the songwriters were asked if there were any factors, traits, or ingredients, we may have omitted that help in becoming a successful, hit songwriter, here are some of their answers: "As in any walk of life, it's not just nurture, it's nature too.", "You can learn a lot about songwriting, and you don't have to be born with it.", "I was given a gift; you can't teach talent. I could spend 40,000 hours practicing basketball and still wouldn't be LeBron James; he's a superhuman, he's on a different level.", "Be a good listener and listen to yourself.", "the desire to make the song you write today better than the one you wrote yesterday," "Having thick skin is the key—never give up.", "Timing and luck is the essence of the whole thing." , "knowing the right people," " Learn to play other instruments well.", "Learn the history of American popular music.", "the willingness to go deeper than the surface in songwriting," "Practice the art of kindness to others.", "You always have to have your antenna up.", "You always have to be looking for new ideas.", "You have to be eaten up with it." and "It's some of the things I talked about before. Like my son; when he goes on the road with me, he plays the keyboard, he's 26 now, he started, maybe doing this when he was 19. He plays maybe six or seven songs with my band. But what I did when he was bringing things up on the computer; I'd maybe show him a chord a day. But when I showed him a chord a day, I wanted him to see what that chord looked like on music paper, and he could see from the music paper, and to know which finger goes where on the keyboard. Some people would find that was boring: "I can just type it into my phone"; but that's not good enough for me. You really have to be well-rounded. Learn how to write music down on a piece of paper."

A majority of those interviewed said songwriters are both born and made. A few of the writers believed birth had very little to do with whether you became a hit songwriter or not. And a few believed a songwriter was solely made. Here are their opinions: "You can have a gift, but you still have to work your ass off to get better and better. ",." Both, it is an innate gift," "It's the Jubal gene.", "Songwriting is a craft that must be learned and constantly practiced.", "I don't think birth has much to do with it." , "Innately given.", "Both born and made.", " I think songwriting is half craft and half talent.", "Made.", and "Talent is given; it is mad and being lucky."

When asked whether a talent is a gift or earned, these are some of the comments we received: "Talent by definition is a gift.", "Some people are gifted., the people who have been the most successful have taken lessor talent and have worked their asses off to develop it.", "This is a very subjective question—we are all born with talents towards many things.", "I think everyone is born with gifts.", " A gift is from God.", "Talent is a gift, but it also be earned.", "Talent is gifted to us by our Creator. What we do with that is up to us.", "It is a gift, and it is earned.", "I do think it is a gift.", "I've seen different writers at different levels of that gift.", "Both, I think it's a gift, but also earned.", "It's a gift. What you do with it is earned." and "Talent has a way of growing. The more time you spend with your muse, the more time you spend with your activity, the more you are involved with it—the talent you are involved in. So, your talent should grow. You should live with it. You'll get bored if you're doing the same thing. Do different things. It is a learning process, a growing process. Nobody wouldn't have given me five cents to be able to say when I was first starting out, that I had any talent—I thought I had none."

On the topic, if talent comes from within, we received the following opinions: "comes from within," "For me, talent comes from thanking Jesus.", "It's a gift from God.", "I believe talent comes from within and is then nurtured from within and without.", "I think we react to stimuli.", " I think talent is God-given. You can either use it or throw it away.", "I think that talent comes from a lot of different sources.", "Talent comes from above and within. It's how you process it."

We received the following different definitions of talent in the songwriter's own words: "Something you are born with that gives you the potential to excel in whatever area or areas.", "Talent is our purpose.", "Maybe, talent is the result of working inhumanely hard to perfect your passion for your craft.", "Ability. I sang before I spoke, I knew I was supposed to sing, I just knew when I was born.", "Talent is digging deep within myself.", "a natural proclivity enhanced by thousands of hours of practice," "The unique excellence that lies in each of us.", "Talent is the capacity to honor an internal endowment of soulful riches, genius and autonomous daring where chances are taken to expand a conversation that would not otherwise be available to the collective.", "When it comes to music, the only test for me is how it makes me feel.", "Talent is this entity that drives us mad sometimes.", "It's a skill learned and mastered to a high level.", "I think Talent is a God-given thing.", "It is what you start with." and "good achievements, good results; there are people who are so talented who are playing in bars in a Holiday Inn somewhere. You've got to be lucky, too."

Most of the songwriters we interviewed believed that self-criticism helped in becoming a hit songwriter. Here are some of their comments: "both helps and hurts," "It hurts if it is self-defeating.", "Self-criticism is an important process in creativity to grow, as long as you keep self-criticism in check.", "It's important early on as a songwriter to turn off the self-editor and let things flow freely, look at the bigger picture." "Self-criticism will help you beat the critics to the punch.", "If "self-criticism" is looked at in a positive way as in "soul-searching" then I do believe yes.", "You have to critique yourself.", "I think it's a device to shoot for higher goals—being a perfectionist.", "It's a double-edged sword.", "Change the self-criticism by removing the self from blindness that keeps you stuck.", "Know the truth about who you are.", "I would change self-criticism to editing.", " It helps, but be objective.", "Constructive self-criticism is good.", "It helps.", "It only harms you if you let it.", "It's crucial without being self-destructive.", and "Yes. I think it help. Okay, now let me hear it again—what's wrong with it, what can I change? You have to be able to try to be the listener."

When asked whether songwriters are more attuned to all that is going around them in this world, we received these remarks: "I don't know.", "There are songwriters who are sensitive and others who could care less about feelings or emotions in a song.", "Everything in a songwriter's life and around the songwriter is material.", "yes," "I believe "Creatives" in general are more attuned to their surroundings absolutely yes.", "Since most songwriters spend their waking hours in a room alone, I doubt they are more attuned than others to the outside world…no.", "Yes, creative people in general are.", "yes and no," " I do believe there are some guys in town who are the "flavor of the month"—everyone is cutting their songs. I think there is a formula, they get onto, and it works for them, yes."

We asked the songwriters if they believed inspiration was a state of mind and if it could be a major factor in the creation of a hit songwriter. Here is what some of them said: "Inspiration is a mystery.", "Inspiration is unexplainable like love.", "Inspiration is for amateurs.", "It is a state of mind." "As a successful, professional songwriter, one must find inspiration in everything.", "yes state of mind," " I tend to write from inspiration." "definitely a state of mind of being curious about the world, about people, about political conversations and listening to what is being said around you," "Inspiration to me is emotional.", "Yes, I go in spurts with ideas.", "Some days everything sounds like a song and some days nothing sounds like a song.", "I wouldn't call it a state of mind, but I think songwriters need to be tuned into their personal "songwriting channel."

We asked the songwriters if they thought having empathy was important to writing hit songs. Here are some of their comments: "Having empathy is a critical thing to have in songwriting," "We have to relate to people to be allowed to sing into their lives.", "It helps in becoming a better human being which might help you become a better songwriter.", "Having empathy helps with everything.", "Songwriters need the ability to see the bigger picture, a rounder picture and be able to empathize with many personalities and situations.", "I feel very strongly about empathy.", "I'm never one to brag about myself, but if I have one quality to talk about, it is that I have deep empathy for the world.", "yes," "There's only time for love in this world so be kind about it when you write.", "I believe empathy makes a better person, but can't see how it's terribly relevant to the creative process.", "What's the difference between empathy and compassion?", "Certainly empathy helps you become a better songwriter." "I do believe in it.", "Empathy comes from deep within. You must care about others and the world.", "Empathy plays a large part in successful songwriting." "Inspiration is a state of mind like being hypnotized or in a trance.", "I think all great songwriters have a sensitive side where they understand what others are going through, whether it be happy or sad.", "I think it can be empathy for others and for yourself." and "Empathy is an essential item to have in whatever you're doing in life—if you're an accountant, or whether you're working in McDonald's. It's essential to have empathy whether you're a songwriter or not."

Chapter Thirty:

Self-Evaluation Questionnaire

Throughout this book, you have read many interviews of highly successful people. Now it's time to think about your career. You have already made the decision to become a songwriter; now how are you going to become a successful songwriter? We have carefully and thoughtfully created questions which are designed make you think critically about yourself and your songwriting. Take your time. You don't have to know every answer right now.

- **How much drive, passion, and stamina (energy level) do you have in working toward becoming a hit songwriter?**
- **Think about your work ethic. What are you doing every day to become a successful hit songwriter?**
- **How much faith and belief in your abilities do you have?**
- **How much focus to detail and perfection do you have in your artistry?**
- **What are your short and long-term goals?**
- **Failure and rejections are part of life and becoming a successful songwriter. How have you learned from failure and rejection or do you believe that everything happens for a reason?**
- **Do you feel like being obsessive and persistent with writing help in becoming a successful, hit songwriter? If so, how?**
- **Do you think taking risks in your career has helped you become successful? How?**
- **Have you missed opportunities because you didn't take a risk? Why didn't you take that risk?**
- **Do you have a positive mental attitude? Do you take that positivity with you everywhere and when you write?**
- **Do you have a tendency to only talk about what you are going to do? Why do you think that is? How can you become more of a doer and not a talker?**
- **Are you a visionary or a dreamer? How does that help you in your songwriting?**
- **Do you think overall personality contributes to the success of a songwriter? If so, how? Think about your personality. Are you someone that people would like to work with?**
- **Do you feel patience and practice play a role in the creation of a hit songwriter? How? Do you have patience in the process of becoming successful in this field?**
- **How much time do you spend prioritizing your life from day-to-day? Do you find yourself only thinking about anything other than your goals of becoming a successful songwriter? Why do you think that is?**
- **How much learning and reading to you do about your desired profession?**
- **How much self-discipline and perseverance do you have in becoming a successful songwriter?**
- **Do you believe a hit songwriter is born or made? Why?**
- **Do you believe talent is a gift or is it earned? Explain your thoughts.**
- **Do you believe that talent comes from within? If so, is it how they process stimuli in life?**
- **What is talent in your own words?**
- **Do you believe self-criticism helps or harms the success of a hit songwriter? Explain.**
- **Do you believe hit songwriters are more attuned to what is going on and happening around them than others? Please elaborate.**
- **Do you believe inspiration is a state of mind and could it be a major factor in the creation of a hit songwriter? Why?**
- **Do you believe having empathy helps in becoming a hit songwriter? Explain.**

Recommended Reading

Bacharach, Burt:
Anyone Who Had a Heart: My Life

Cline, Thornton:
Practice Personalities for Adults

Coyle, Daniel:
The Talent Code

Davis, Sheila:
The Songwriter's Idea Book

Gilbert, Elizabeth:
Big Magic

Gladwell, Malcom:
Outliers

L. Ron Hubbard:
Art

Hall. Tom T:
The Songwriter's Handbook

Josefs, Jai:
Writing Music for Hit Songs

King, Stephen:
On Writing

Murphy, Ralph:
Murphy's Laws of Songwriting: The Book

Nathan, Edy:
It's Grief: The Dance of Self-Discovery Through Trauma and Loss

Pressfield, Stephen:
The War of Art

Selke, Michael:
Nashville Cat: The Wayne Moss Story

Smith/Ashford and Simpson:
You're All I Need to Get By

Vandiver, Jerry and Holcombe, Gracie:
Your First Cut: A Step-by-Step Guide to Getting There

Webb, Jimmy:
Inside the Art of Songwriting

About The Authors

Author/Artist/Songwriter, and Multi-Instrumentalist, **Lacie Carpenter**

Hailing from Texas and graduating from Stephen F. Austin University with her degree in Music Education/ specialization in Violin Performance and an MS in Psychology--Lacie teaches private lessons in many musical genres, writing courses, and is an adjunct psychology professor. She performs globally with other artists and her one-woman show. With her 4 string acoustic violin and her 7-string fretted, Mark Wood Viper (The Beast,) and her eclectic vocal stylings—from concert halls to house concerts... she puts on quite the show. She has performed internationally with 9 symphonies, chamber orchestras, choirs, symphonic bands, and solo acts. She had the great honor of performing for the Arch-Bishop and Prime Minister of Austria. Lacie studied with Dr. Jennifer Dalmas, Dr. Isidor Saslav and Dr. Jane Saber. For 7 years, she built orchestra programs in Texas before moving to Nashville, TN to pursue her many ambitions. Lacie is an active songwriter, author, session player, arranger, blogger, educator, and church choir member.

About the Authors

She is the winner of 12 East Texas Music Awards, but the ones she is most proud of are: Fiddler Of The Year 2012-2014, 2016 and 2017. In 2015, Lacie was awarded ETX Bluegrass Act of the Year.

Lacie has been able to grace the stage with greats such as Mark O'Connor, Mark Wood, Judy Hyman, Jonna Fitzgerald, Bruce Molsky, Isidor Saslav, and Jimmy Fortune. Her first album, "Nothing is Real," debuted in October 2018 and was produced by Wayne Moss. She is also the fiddler for Jerry Vandiver. Her first novel, AKA which she co-wrote with Thornton Cline, hit the shelves early 2019.

Author, songwriter, educator, instrumentalist, **Thornton Cline**

Ever since his mother signed him up for piano lessons, Thornton Cline has been writing non-stop. With over 1,000 published songs, 150 recorded songs, twenty-six adult, YA and children's books published, Thornton Cline has been nominated multiple times for Grammy and Dove Awards. Cline has been honored with "Songwriter of the Year" twice-in-a-row and received a platinum certified award for sales of over one million album units in Europe. He won the first place Maxy Literary Award 2017 for "Children's Young Adult Book", and has had his songs recorded by Engelbert Humperdinck, Gloria Gaynor, Rebecca Holden, Gary Puckett, Tim Murphy, Ray Peterson, Tammy Trent, Billy and Sarah Gaines, Matt Newton among others. Many of Cline's tunes have appeared in the top of the charts.

Cline continues to mentor, teach and inspire aspiring authors and songwriters all around the world as CEO/president of his publishing company, Clinetel Music. Cline is a regular speaker and moderator at the Winter and Summer NAMM shows, an in-demand speaker as well in the United States at libraries, colleges, schools and conventions. He is a faculty member of Cumberland University, Sumner Academy and Welch College.